Sex, Love and the
Dangers of Intimacy

Sex, Love and the Dangers of Intimacy

A Guide to Passionate Relationships
When the 'Honeymoon' Period is Over

Helena Løvendal and Nick Duffell

Thorsons

Thorsons
An Imprint of HarperCollins*Publishers*
77–85 Fulham Palace Road
Hammersmith, London w6 8JB

The Thorsons website address is:
www.thorsons.com

and *Thorsons*
are trademarks of
HarperCollins*Publishers* Limited

Published by Thorsons 2002

10 9 8 7 6 5 4 3 2 1

© Helena Løvendal and Nick Duffell 2002

Helena Løvendal and Nick Duffell assert the moral
right to be identified as the author of this work

A catalogue record for this book is available
from the British Library

ISBN 0 00 710089 2

Printed and bound in Great Britain by
Creative Print and Design Wales, Ebbw Vale

To the next generations

CONTENTS

Part 4: New Life

Acknowledgements

It is a pleasure to get to the end and to be allowed to thank those who have helped us on this project.

First, thanks are due to all the couples we have worked with over the years in therapy and on the workshops. They have continually shown us both how hard the path of conscious relationship is, but that such a vision can still grow corn.

Secondly, we wish to thank those who have supported and challenged us during our own 'dancing in the dark', especially Beckett Ender, Ben Fuchs, Frankie McMahon, Nick Dawson, Nick Hedley, Mandakini Hildequist, Punit Fischer, Reinhard Kowalski, Rob Bland, Surabhi Schubmeyer and Veronica Houghton. We do not wish to omit Inge Johanssen, nor Joy and the late Paddy Duffell. We could not have made any sense of it without your help.

Next, we owe thanks to the teachers we have been lucky enough to have been apprenticed to – Danielle Roux, Harley SwiftDeer Reagan and Willem Poppeliers, as well as to our supervisor and mentor, John Hale.

We also wish to express our gratitude to those teachers and writers we have learned most from, notably Arnold Mindell, Bernadette Jacot, Clarissa Pinkola Estes, Hal Stone, Ken Wilber, Liam Hudson, Malidoma Somé, Marion Woodman, Robert Bly, Sidra Winkleman and Subonfu Somé.

We must not forget to thank our erstwhile colleagues at the Institute of Psychosynthesis, nor our co-workers on the Contextual Couple Counselling training at ReVison, both in London. We also want to say thank you to our outrageous colleagues on the first Sexual Grounding Therapy training in the Netherlands and Mexico.

Finally, huge gratitude is due to Reinhard Kowalski for reading and commenting on nearly every word of the first draft of the manuscript and to our editor at HarperCollins, Carole Tonkinson, who commissioned the book and skilfully guided the final draft into place.

Thanks to you all!

Helena and Nick

Jouqueviel, Summer 2001

Credits

'A Marriage', by Robert Creeley, from *Collected Poems of Robert Creeley, 1945–1975,* © 1983 The Regents of the University of California, is used by kind permission of the University of California Press.

'Advice', from *The Dead Get by with Everything* (Minneapolis: Milkweed Editions, 1990), © 1990 Bill Holm, is reprinted with permission from Milkweed Editions, www.milkweed.org.

'First Degree Marriage', from *After the Merrymaking* (Jonathan Cape, London, 1971) is reprinted by permission of PDF on behalf of Roger McGough. © Roger McGough as printed in the original volume.

Extracts from *About a Boy* by Tony Parsons are reproduced by kind permission of HarperColinsPublishers Ltd.

I've got you under my skin, words and music by Cole Porter, © 1973 Chappell Co., Inc., assigned to Buxton Hill Music Corp., USA, Warner/ Chappell Music Ltd, London W6 8BS, reproduced by permission of International Music Publications Ltd. All rights reserved.

'The Dream' by Felix Pollak from *Subject to Change*, Juniper Press, 1978, © Sara Pollak, is reprinted by kind permission of Juniper Press.

You've Lost That Lovin' Feelin', words and music by Barry Mann, Cynthia Weil and Phil Spector, © 1964, 1965 (renewed 1992, 1993) Screen Gems-EMI Music, Inc., and Mother Bertha Music, Inc. Administered by ABKCO Music, Inc. All rights reserved, international copyright secured, used by permission.

'Listening to the Köln Concert' and 'A Man and a Woman Sit Near Each Other' from *Loving a Woman in Two Worlds*, by Robert Bly,

About This Book

This is a book about love. Or rather, it is a book about daring to learn how to love. It explains why people wh fall in love so often seem to end up as sources of hurt and disappointment for each other, rather than of joy and fulfilment. It's a book that explores why the greatest sources of power within human beings – love and sexual energy – can create so much havoc in relationships and families all over the world. It suggests that there are ways to harness this energy for untold benefit.

Our principal thesis is that conflict *inevitably* arises when partners come together in a sexual relationship, and that it cannot be avoided. It is like a chemical process. The joining of male and female energies invokes a deep and universal pattern that has unparalleled power. If we understand how to tap its creative alchemy, we may flower, otherwise it can destroy us.

These days, when couples experience the difficulties of relationship they tend to think it was all a big mistake and more often than not separate. Until quite recently, people tended to grit their teeth and bear it instead. This book offers an alternative approach. It suggests that there are very specific pathways through relationship conflict and that such a journey, if bravely and creatively undertaken, can offer an unparalleled route to individual transformation. However, in order for true intimacy to start to flow naturally between partners, each partner's immature identity has to be destroyed in the process.

None of this is easy. Nor does society's dependence on the 'feel-good factor' encourage such a view. When couples run into difficulty they often feel failures and very alone. African shaman Malidoma Somé says that relationship is too much for one couple to bear alone, for there is too much Spirit in it. It takes a village to support them. Our hope is that this book will provide some support for those who are curious about the challenge of intimate relationships as well as for those who cannot yet see any light in the darkness of their disappointment.

Some of what we say in this book may be new to you, though much may strike a chord of recognition. We hope that our approach is refreshing, but we do not claim any particular originality. Our work is largely a synthesis and whatever we present that appears to be true has most likely already been discovered by others – because it works. However, this is a book written from the inside out and we are passionate about what we say. What we have learned about the dynamics of relationship comes from our own life experience – primarily through our own struggle. We wrote this book because we have lived it.

To this we add what we have learned from counselling many couples in crisis. A most important ingredient has been the experience of meeting couples in our 'A Man and a Woman' workshop programme and later the training of 'Contextual Couple Counsellors'.

In the workshops and training courses we give we are very visible as a couple and as individuals with our different styles. We share much of our story. Here we have chosen to expose ourselves a little less. We also wanted to protect the couples we have worked with. For this reason we decided not to use 'case studies'. Instead, we introduce a fictional archetypal couple and later their friends. Their stories illustrate some of the ups and downs of relationship.

The book is divided into four parts. In the first we give an overview and in the second we tackle the difficult subjects of despair, stuckness and conflict. The third introduces a new way of looking at universal and cultural issues of difference between men and women; the fourth speaks about the Soul of couplehood.

In writing, we have chosen to forgo the attempt to find a joint voice. We could not do it anyway, for we do not agree on every single matter – after all, we are a man and a woman! So we began the chapters on our own and then each was editor to the other. It has been an interesting process!

Similarly, because we have approached this subject from the inside, we have focused exclusively on heterosexual relationships. We know that this may disappoint those who are interested in other forms. But our decision was entirely pragmatic – we have tried to concentrate on what we know best, rather than speculating. Internal dynamics such as the Pushme-Pullyou and the 'bonding patterns' will be applicable in all cases anyway, since they have a less strong gender component.

We have not separated chapters on sex from those on relationship. This is because we believe that emotional, psychological and sexual issues are inseparable. Our society has an insatiable fascination with sex, but it covers a profound ignorance. This book is not full of explicit sexual instructions. However, the crucial steps towards an ultimately satisfying and rejuvenating sexual relationship are set out here. There is a reason for this. What we hear from talking to Tantra teachers who are giving the most sophisticated sexual instructions is that the kind of issues which we tackle in this book invariably present themselves and sabotage sexual intimacy. We are not surprised. We found that it was so in our own lives. Sex has been one of the issues where we have encountered most conflict and hurt, and, in the end, the most learning. We discovered that when we address the trouble in our minds and develop new ways of opening our fearful hearts, our bodies know how to make love.

Besides, in matters of sex, gender issues abound. For example, for men, why does sex often seem to be a precursor to intimacy and sometimes a necessary condition? And is it simply one of life's frustrations that for women the opposite appears to be true: that relational intimacy is a gateway into their being genuinely open for sex? There seem to be some general principles to understand here. Despite the risk of oversimplification, or of offending those who want everyone to be the same or who say everything is socially determined, we have decided to have our say, in the knowledge that – as storyteller Michael Meade has commented – whenever you speak about gender you run into trouble.

The point is that if you really engage in the passion of intimate relationships you just can't avoid 'trouble'.

But you probably know that already, or you wouldn't have picked up this book.

PART 1
For Better or Worse

CHAPTER 1

A Man and a Woman –
the Impossible Alchemy?

Love is the chaos theory of human relationships. Daily life seems fairly lawful, organised around certain routines or principles, and then along comes love and changes everything.

Susan Edwards[1]

The lights went out and the lock on the office door made a satisfying 'clunk'. We reached the bottom of the stairs and opened the door onto the street. A big red bus hurtled round the corner into the city night. We were on our way home after a long day of seeing clients in our therapy practice. We were tired, but feeling good.

For the last hour we had been working together, seeing a couple. Like many other couples before them they had entered the waiting room shyly, as if they were afraid someone they knew might see them. They looked ashamed as they walked up the stairs to our consulting room, as if they felt themselves to be failures, as if they imagined that they shouldn't be in need of help. As always, we tried to reassure them in some way, because we know – from personal as well as from professional experience – that being in a couple is not easy.

When we started counselling we had completed an extensive and expensive training programme. We had been thoroughly supervised, had read exquisite texts on the art. We knew how to see the soul in a person, not just the symptoms. But when we began to work in a counselling clinic we were quite unprepared for what came our way. Almost every case involved issues of relationship or sexual problems and the management was desperate for its workers to see couples. But we had had no training in relationship work and so we had to learn it on the hoof and get extra training as we went along. We made some awful mistakes, but we had some successes too. A breakthrough occurred when we began to work together as a couple and to be honest about what we were thinking and feeling. So we began to develop our own style and method.

On the night in question, some five years after we had started, we felt good about the work we had done with that particular couple. Like others before them, they were not having sex and had not had any for a while. They were full of disappointment, which readily turned to blame. We had been able to help them both to step into the shoes of the other for a while, and some compassion and understanding had been re-leased. With our prompting they had been able to realize that their relationship might be poised to reach for another level and that this was in fact quite alarming for both of them. All four of us had left the room that night with tender and tenta-tive smiles on our faces.

But here's the rub. By the time these heroic counsellors had found their car and driven half a mile on the way to their home a topic had arisen which had brought forth a few short-tempered remarks and then an icy silence.

We felt like failures. And worse: hypocrites.

Elusive Intimacy

To work as a psychotherapist is a great privilege. Not only do you get a chance of helping someone and being paid for it, but through the window of their story you also get endless chances for insights into the problems of life. We had worked with many couples in crisis and probably did some good. We were both psychotherapists, trainers and workshop leaders, supposedly experts at communication and listening, but *at home* it was a different story.

Let us come clean and admit right from the start that neither of us has found anything in life more challenging than the process of being emotionally and sexually intimate with another human being. Despite being in and out of therapy and psychological training since the early eighties nothing has provoked us or evoked as much of our 'stuff' as the task of intimate relationship. Why should this be so? Don't we all long to be connected to another human being through love, friendship and sex?

There are several quick answers. First, men and women are so different. And as for intimacy itself? Deep inside we have had to admit that although the longing for intimacy is genuine, it also terrifies us and sometimes even repels us. It is so damn hard and seems to mean giving up so much. There is nothing in our upbringing that prepares us for it – except the models that our own families provided us with. But mostly these models only help us to grin and bear it or, more subtly, as we shall see, instruct us in how to protect ourselves from the other.

Despite all our training and working as divorce mediators, couple counsellors and individual therapists, our own failures at conscious intimate relationship with a committed partner were too hard to ignore. But of course mostly we believed it was the fault of the other. It stared us in the face – and we were only too happy to reflect those omissions back, loudly and clearly.

Between us we had three failed marriages. In order for us to be together Nick had left his first wife and thereby created chaos in the lives of his two sons, and Helena had left her second husband less than a year after their wedding. After a brief period, when we were floating on a cloud of love, a grim reality began to settle in. We found that we were doing little else but alternating between furious arguments or civil frigidity, and bringing out the worst aspects of each other. Two therapists in conflict is not a pretty sight: each is convinced of the other's pathology! God knows what the neighbours thought. We started to fear we had thrown everything away for this torture. What had once been a dream was now turning into a nightmare.

Our 'honeymoon period' – the carefree time when an intimate relationship focuses exclusively on the good things and has yet to engage the difficulties – was probably shorter than normal, due to the added strain of becoming a step-family. We now know that a step-family is a heavy reality which permits very little room for romantic dreaming. But initially we felt strong enough to conquer any obstacle. Today, as more families are breaking up, an increasing number of partners face this problem as they re-enter relationships. In a step-family it is practically impossible to get it right for all the members all the time and almost certain that you will get it wrong for most of the members most of the time. Nor is it easy to say for whom it is worse. The step-parent can feel excluded and on trial. The children feel confused and only want it never to have happened. The original parent feels guilty and tries to make it up to all sides, but easily ends up making a mess of everything. At least that is how it was for us.

A step-family is a situation that puts enormous stress on all concerned. And people tend to revert to primitive survival tactics when under stress. Unfortunately, as our beloved is the one closest to us, we tend to let off the steam that this stress has generated in their direction. Where once we experienced closeness, warmth, love, support, care and safety, now we see only anger, hatred, mistrust, betrayal and deep pain. When this kind of thing happens it is hard to remember that these horrible feelings are also part of intimacy. For us, it became increasingly difficult to remember the good qualities we once saw in each other. What now stared us in the face were the 'true' aspects of our lover: the selfishness, the pride and all those once minor irritants which could no longer be ignored.

Why didn't we give up then? Perhaps because it happened so fast that we still remembered the love between us ... perhaps because we thought we owed it to the children, who had already suffered from the break-up of their family ... perhaps because we were too exhausted to run off and try again. Probably it was a mixture of all of them put together.

Eventually, after some time, when the discomfort had settled in and become *the* pattern that we returned to again and again, we had a moment of sanity and curiosity. We looked at one another and asked the obvious question: 'What *is* going on?' We knew from our work that the challenge of intimacy had many people beaten. Many were resigned or dared not hope for more than they already had. We looked around at our friends and colleagues and the picture was very much the same. It wasn't really working for anyone. Divorce rates, single-parent statistics and the ubiquitous lonely-hearts columns seemed to confirm the notion that we were not alone. 'It can't *just* be us!' we protested.

Then we remembered a joke – a story about an innocent child shovelling manure in a stable. The child had a bubble above his head that read: 'With all this shit there must be a pony in here somewhere!'

That was the trigger. We began to question whether our relationship trouble was something we were *meant* to run into. Could it be that rather than heading for failure we were revealing things about ourselves and about the nature of intimacy which could only be achieved through the medium of extreme discomfort? Was it possible that this conflict actually had some purpose? More or less everyone we knew seemed to be in trouble in their relationships, though some couples seemed to actively pursue the avoidance of conflict, while others seemed to be addicted to it. Was it possible that this was the same dynamic in different forms?

Alright, but if conflict was *meant* to be there, then what on earth was it there *for*? Could it be that evoking these unsavoury self-pitying, maligned parts of ourselves was what the relationship wanted in order to transform us? Could there exist such an entity as 'The Relationship' which actually had a healing potential? Or was this just wishful thinking? If it were true, could there ever be lasting happiness? We could not be sure of anything, but we began to be interested and to search through psychology books, and myths, and stories to see if there was any ancient or modern evidence for such a theory.

During those moments of sanity when we tried to consider such questions, we began to have a little compassion for the task of relationship. It began to look as if there was some outrageous process at work which could invite death into a relationship. What seemed to be dying were two things: first, the idea of a love which could conquer any obstacle, and second, the attractive images which we once had of one another. The first was too difficult to contemplate at that time because we still felt sorry for ourselves. But the second seemed very perverse and quite specific.

We had already realized that many of the very things that had attracted us to one another were becoming sources of intense irritation. For example, Helena's optimistic and relaxed attitude to life once held great allure for Nick. He had been brought up in a regimented, boarding-school way of dealing with time and had initially loved how 'laid back' Helena was. But soon he became preoccupied with how she consistently

kept him waiting and was *never* on time for anything! This
began to drive him absolutely crazy. Meanwhile Helena had
initially regarded Nick's ability to discriminate, make decisions
and act on them as an attractive masculine bonus. Now she
began to feel totally controlled by him!

And worse, as we began to make less effort to attract one
another, we saw ourselves becoming possessed by family
demons. Nick found himself acting the familiar tyrant he had
sworn he had left behind in the person of his father, and magically began to resemble Helena's controlling and abandoning
father. As he did so, he felt deprived of Helena's loving understanding – just the maternal care he had always craved. In fact
Helena was transforming into a furious witch in front of his
eyes. As Nick witnessed this, a chilling yet familiar sensation
would come over him.

It was as if each partner had the power to evoke the most
unpleasant, uncooperative side of the other. And that seemed
partly to be the point. Mostly we are unaware of having such
difficult aspects of our personalities – or unwilling to admit
them. But we found that to retain any integrity, the one in
whom they were evoked could no longer continue as if they did
not exist. In this way, perversely, each partner's complaint
seemed to be a service to the other. And so we began to discover some of the ways in which the relationship was provoking us to refine ourselves. We were being forced to face and
acknowledge parts of ourselves which we did not show in other
areas of our lives or could even recognize as part of ourselves.

Gradually it began to dawn on us that the relationship conflict was inviting us into a process of death. We were dying to
our own self-images and to the images we had of each other.
But there was a light at the end of the tunnel. This was not the
end of the story, but an organic process, a part of the cycle of
life that leads to death, which in turn leads to new life. It was
therefore a part of the fundamental laws of nature.

It seemed as if this cycle had a purpose, embodied by a principle, which was outside the two of us. It could remain true even when we found ourselves in the grip of the conflict and unable to hold onto the idea. Its purpose seemed to be to present us with disowned parts of ourselves in order for us to fully integrate them. Ultimately, thus fully committed to ourselves, we might become more whole and then, paradoxically more able to renounce our beliefs about ourselves, we might become free to properly commit to each other.

This outrageous cycle had reached places in us that therapy had failed to penetrate. It seemed as if its nature was 'feminine' and chaotic, frightening and healing; it reminded us of the description of the Indian goddess Kali, renowned for wielding power over life and death. Despite her terrifying appearance, she is said to be compassionate and kills only in order to create new and better life.

Attempting to ride the bilious waves of conscious relationship takes stamina and courage, but our growing understanding helped us regain respect for ourselves and for each other. Our trembling hearts slowly began to reopen towards each other. We started to relate to each other from a different level.

Nevertheless, not all our learned behaviour and fears suddenly melted away. We recognized that in order to let this chaos happen between us, we needed stronger boundaries. It was no longer enough just to stay together as long as it felt OK. Most of the time it did not feel OK. We recognized that our emotional life, though important, was so ephemeral that to give over the command of our destiny to it seemed reckless. After all, feelings are simply energy on the loose – repressing them is dangerous, but so is not containing them. We decided that we needed to get married.

And that's when all the fans in the stable suddenly turned fully on – and there was manure everywhere!

Learning from Birds, Bees and Flowers

In Denmark, where Helena was born, they speak of the process of love as 'the bees and the flowers'. The delicious experience of falling in love resembles how flowers attract bees with their seductive fragrance. Yet falling in love, or finding the flowers, is but the initial stage of the art of making honey.

Human beings are complex and multifaceted. Torn by seemingly conflicting needs and longings, we struggle to integrate the different aspects within ourselves. Had Nature decided to wait for individuals to be 'sorted' before releasing the fragrance of the sexual urges, the species wouldn't have survived. So she plays a very beautiful trick: we fall in love. Then we fall out – it's the next stage, and it hurts. The logic is clear: the strength of the attraction determines the strength of repulsion.

We were now fully committed to one another, but we still couldn't manage the differences between us. Like winter following summer, we had fallen out of love and into disappointment. 'You are not who I thought you were...' 'This is not how I wanted us to turn out...' 'If this is what we do to each other, we can't be right for one another...' In our painful isolation, such thoughts went around and around inside our heads.

It may come as no surprise that our sex life suffered. What had been vigorous exciting exchanges when we first met were now occasions of endless conflict. Sex became a medium where emotional issues invariably surfaced. Our attempts to manage the difficulties of sexual intimacy – whether by avoidance or indulgence – failed. Eventually, we could not ignore what we began to see.

In a relationship where sex is never withheld, conflict may be minimized and this helps partners – especially the men – feel good about themselves. But often such an unspoken arrangement involves a deal for the sake of security and enables both partners to avoid relational intimacy. On the other hand, in our relationship, Nick was forever pushing for sex, while Helena was hard to get. In consequence Nick found her even more attractive and felt cursed by an ironical god as his frustration increased. In this way we avoided the security collusion but created a perverse system which we only understood later. We had discovered the laws of what we now call 'the Chase' and the phenomenon we call 'the Pushme-Pullyou'.

This next period was the hardest. We were recognizing a lot of patterns but were as yet powerless to alter them. Our sexual difficulties were like a magnifying glass onto these dynamics. They uncovered a mine of information, but our suffering and bewilderment prevented us from putting it to any real use at the time. Instead, yielding to temptations from outside the relationship seemed a very attractive option. Eventually, we were forced to realize that dealing openly with the pain between us was the only chance we had to salvage what was left of our love.

In the process we learned how easily the sexual energies can be hijacked by unresolved emotional issues. Thus a couple can end up in an arena where it becomes nearly impossible to recognize the real problems before too much pain is caused and any remaining trust broken. We became curious to explore the power of sexuality. Enrolling as students on various training courses took us further down the road of what was to become a great adventure.

We had not yet understood the nature of what we now know as 'bonding patterns', though we were deeply in their grip. But recognizing such dynamics in our sex life lifted the lid on many interactions we were prone to. Bonding patterns will be discussed at length in subsequent chapters. In essence they are patterns in which the Inner Parent part in each partner bonds or spars with the Inner Child part in the other. This unwitting bonding is a principal ingredient in the initial attraction between couples. It becomes the dynamic basis of most arguments and forms patterns of relating which can last a lifetime.

On reflection, we can now analyse part of our initial attraction to another in the following way. Nick had originally fallen in love with a 'good mother' part in Helena which could genuinely listen to and nourish the 'needy child' in him. In his previous marriage he had repressed this part by playing the role of the one who held it all together. Of course there was a pay-off for this. The bottom line was that he was more comfortable and less vulnerable with such a self-image. But it was an illusion which had to die. For Helena's part, she had heard Nick say he would never abandon his children and the conscious part of her supported the integrity of this decision. However, the 'little girl' in her concluded that finally here was a man who wouldn't desert her as her father had done. In effect, she ended up playing second fiddle to Nick's children, once more cast as the 'caretaker without needs' in the family, a role which she knew well from her own family of origin. She had to learn to acknowledge her own needs in order to free her power, instead of exchanging it for a promise of love.

Love, Loss and Longing

We were learning, but we were still hurt and disappointed. At the same time, our hearts and bodies were full of yearning for connection and grief at the loss of what had once been. But we both felt far too vulnerable to stay with this simple fact for very long. A wrong look or a carelessly uttered word would throw us back into conflict and endless draining arguments.

If two people reach this point and there is nothing, such as children, marriage or joint finance, to hold them together, the only sensible action seems to be to end the relationship and search for honey elsewhere – all too often only to repeat the same story over again. If there are factors preventing a fast getaway, a relationship can descend into patterns of resignation or resentment. Although these can prove amazingly durable, without mutual love or joy they are simply a dead-end street.

Often we felt we were getting nowhere, but sometimes we began to see ourselves as being in a process of giving birth to a third entity – a presence unique to our relationship. Then we were each able to consider the failings of the other as more than irritants to put up with and could relate to them as never-ceasing opportunities to learn more about the disowned or unconscious parts of ourselves. For example, Nick would begin to question what had happened to his own 'laid-back' part. Helena would question why she needed Nick to be strong when in reality she was no longer a child but a very competent and powerful adult woman. These realizations did not detract from Nick's genuine strength, nor from Helena's trusting attitude to life, but added value to the overall qualities of the relationship. For the more partners are able to integrate of themselves, the richer a relationship becomes.

But first we had to learn that the kind of defeated resignation where you withdraw and get on with life the best you know how – tempting as it was – just wouldn't do. What eventually allowed us to do more than just survive this stage was learning to grieve the apparent loss of love – together. So much energy had gone into blaming each other for the pain and fear we experienced: 'If you would only stop/do more of ... then everything would be as it used to be,' and so on. We were each desperately trying to change the other. Meanwhile, our relationship itself, like a *Third Being*, was nudging us to change ourselves and give up the focus on the other.

It is hard to face the death of the illusion of the partner as the perfect other. Poet Robert Bly puts it perfectly:

When men and women come together,
how much they have to abandon! Wrens
make their nest of fancy threads
and string ends, animals

abandon all their money each year.
What is it that men and women leave?
Harder than wrens' doing, they have
to abandon their longing for the perfect.

The inner nest not made by instinct
will never be quite round,
and each has to enter the nest
made by the other imperfect bird.[2]

Abandoning the 'longing for the perfect' in the other is a profound lesson. Rather than fleeing the other's nest, we had to learn to abandon not only the images that we had of ourselves and of each other, but also of what we had supposed love to be. A crucial element in this was letting go of the fantasy that someone else had the ability to make us happy and feel good about ourselves. It was the start of accepting responsibility for our own lives and became an opening to grow in real love for each other.

Wiser after the Event

There's no such thing as safe love. All attempts to establish a genuine connection with another human being involve risk – the risk of revealing ourselves, getting to know ourselves, sharing our feelings, accepting our vulnerability. All these are exceedingly difficult to do. Learning to love involves revealing to ourselves that what we feel matters, even if it makes us vulnerable and gives a sense of losing control; then we have to make the other's reality as important as our own. This can be more difficult for men than for women, who sometimes tend to overdo it. The challenge for women is often more about accepting their power while letting their feelings guide rather than control them. How individuals deal with such risks has direct implications for the quality of the relationship.

In our story, the pain and disillusionment which we had initially regarded as signs of failure and desperately wished to avoid turned out to be our teachers. We started to be certain that 'the Relationship' had its own existence as a 'Third Being' with needs and purpose, but that it required nurturing and maintenance if it was to become the container which would sustain us. Getting married from a position of lost *naïveté* really made a difference to us.

So what have we learned? We have learned that the pursuit of genuine intimacy is scary and dangerous, since the barriers each person puts up to stay safe, barriers which were designed to last a lifetime, have to be willingly lowered to let the other in. Pursuing a relationship consciously therefore means taking on a huge task – a task that takes more than love. It also takes courage and attention, and above all commitment, plus the ability to let go of the notion of being a failure again and again and again. In short, an intimate relationship is a minefield. Why should anyone take the risk?

At the time when we were diving into books to try to understand what was going on for us we came upon the concept of relationship as teacher, or spiritual path. This seems to be an age-old concept, esoterically adhered to in certain streams of both Eastern and Western schools of philosophy and spirituality. We find ourselves in broad agreement with this notion. However, what we could not find in books is the message that teachers don't come much tougher than this one!

It is tempting to write from a resolved position, recounting the terrors of one's adventures from a safe distance. But of course we don't have all the answers and it is important for us not to give the impression that there is a once-and-for-all solution or state to attain. We have gone through changes unimaginable to us 15 years ago, when we first naïvely committed to 'doing it differently this time'. Yet we cannot pretend that everything is sorted and cleared between us. It is not. We are still actively participating in the processes we describe. Friends and colleagues who have witnessed some of these processes know that there's nothing enlightened about us when we dive into the next wave of lessons on this path.

Nevertheless, or perhaps because of that, our sense of awe never ceases as we witness the ways in which our relationship continues to reveal to us our deepest and most secret nature. And what allows us to dare share what we have learned is the belief that if *we* can reach the degree of joy and fulfilment that is now a constant undercurrent of our life together, then everybody can. What we have learned has made a great difference to our ability to tolerate what happens between us in the difficult times and to generate enough compassion towards ourselves and each other to increasingly enjoy the good times. In the meantime the bad times get shorter!

Our purpose in this book is to describe the process of transformation which can take place in a long-term committed relationship. But we also want to give an account of what it *feels* like to go through this. Not only do we want to describe the stages that most couples are destined to go through if they stay together for an extended period, but also to acknowledge how terrifying and lonely it can be and how futile it can all seem at times. We were encouraged to know that others experience remarkably similar problems. Many couples don't share this knowledge and they often end up 'dancing in the dark' – or in the divorce courts.

Our hope is that as you read this book you will recognize some of your struggles and sorrows as you do the best you can in the bewildering task of learning to love another soul. We hope that you will be reassured and empowered to know that you are not alone – that your partnership is not the only one in the thick of the fray. And, of course, we hope to persuade some of you that it might be worthwhile hanging on in there. If sometimes – which can begin to feel like *all* the time – it doesn't seem as if you are any good for each other, we would like you to consider that you might be *just perfect* for each other. It may be that it is the perfect fit that hurts.

We see the task of such a relationship rather like yoga: it can stretch and strengthen you if you are committed to practise; it hurts if you don't. We see the pursuit of intimacy and of gender awareness and the practice of conscious sexuality as a transformative path. Claiming our true natures as men and women is a means of bringing soul into the world. Following this path does not necessarily lead to comfort. But it can lead to equality, peace, partnership and the delicious blending of opposites – a celebration of the endless flow of tumbling Yin and Yang.

CHAPTER 2
Irretrievably Broken Down?

If it were a virus that was attacking marriages, epidemiological studies and laboratory research would proceed apace, and public health and public education measures could expect adequate government support.

That is exactly what has happened in the case of AIDS, and rightly so. The incidence of marriage breakdown is in its own way a catastrophe: it demands some priority too.

The Times[1]

Statistics from the end of the twentieth century revealed that close to every other marriage in Britain and America was destined for divorce, while more than half of all cohabiting couples with children were destined to have split up by the time their child was five.[2] The demand for divorce now exceeds the courts' ability to service it.

The social and economic consequences of this trend are pronounced. The largest growing social group is the single household – currently 16 per cent of total households in Britain and projected to be almost 50 per cent by 2010. The demand for single-household housing far outstrips supply and the budgets of those concerned, but, as Denise Knowles of Relate, formerly the Marriage Guidance Agency, told the *Guardian* in September 2000:

Separate households will be increasingly common as women gain financial independence and have less incentive to split the rent.[3]

Clearly there is an epidemic crisis of confidence besieging not only marriage but the very concept of committed relationships. This can be interpreted in various ways. Many factors have clearly taken their toll: the increasing wealth and security of the post-war period, the sexual revolution of the sixties, the changing status of women, the success of 'you-can-have-it-all-and-pay-later' consumerism, to name but a few. The radical developments of the last few decades have rocked the foundations of the rigid authoritarian structures at political, social, economic and religious levels. Much of this authoritarianism was due for a challenge. But it is not only the rigid structures that have had to give way. The West has all but lost the backstop of the extended family with its sense of community, traditions and spiritual roots which once provided an experience of stability, depth and balance.

Increased freedom is the pay-off of these rapid changes, with stress and chaos as the side-effects. But the psyche, which passes on its nature over generations, moves at a slower pace. Our psyches have hardly had time to catch up with life in the twentieth century. We do not yet know what the new way may be, but it is clear that what we have no longer works. Not surprisingly, the nature and future of intimate relationships is up for grabs.

It may be worthwhile, however, not simply to regard the current crisis as something gone wrong. Every crisis brings with it the possibility for change, and often a change is needed, and can be for the best. A panic-driven rush to restore the status quo won't do, for it risks crushing whatever new is attempting to emerge. The chaos might prove fertile, as men and women experiment with new and different lifestyles in the search for a more expanded model of living together. At the same time, we cannot avoid the effects of this problem, for the break-up of family life as we know it also hurts: for many it produces real fear, misery and expense. It affects the very fabric upon which much of our collective identity is based. It therefore demands our full attention.

Marriage and committed relationships have traditionally been entered into on the basis of a more or less explicit sexual contract, which in turn were based on notions of gender. In the attempt to liberate us, our brave new world has turned our previous ideas of sex and gender roles upside-down, while at the same time our lives are saturated with mass-media images of sex and the body beautiful, in the attempt to exploit us. We have lots of possibilities, but we are not quite sure who we are supposed to be.

In this new atmosphere of endless choice anything seems feasible. For example, recent reports from New York tell us of a trend in which couples prefer to share living arrangements with partners of the opposite gender while choosing to have sex with same gender partners outside the home. Indeed, Western Europe and the USA are currently witnessing a trend where couples increasingly opt out of the difficulties of living together while retaining a sense of being in a relationship. Jan Trost, a sociologist from the University of Uppsala in Sweden, says that such couples are now a recognized phenomenon known as 'LAT' – Living Apart Together.[4]

So, if marriage or committed relationships are no longer the prerequisite for status, respectability and financial security, or the only means for women to leave their parental homes or to have babies, nothing is certain. The determining question now is: If it doesn't feel good, why bother?

To begin to answer that question, we have to go back and consider how people managed in the first half of the twentieth century.

Managing the Tension of Opposites

The old model basically provided two options. First there was an ideal of love as portrayed by Hollywood. All it required was an ever-beautiful lover with whom affection and sexual passion was on tap 24 hours a day. Love was all that mattered and any major deviation from this picture inevitably meant that the end was near. Closer to home, the second option involved a practical partnership of finding someone, setting up home, raising a family and making the best of what you had. Sometimes that worked out – with all credit and benefit to the people involved. When it didn't, people's lives could be devastated and the children from such a union were left to make sense of the messages they were given about love, partnership and marriage. These polarized options left behind a legacy to be dealt with.

Opposites are part of our existence – day and night, good and bad, light and dark, life and death, male and female. Each difference contains possibilities as well as limitations. One gives meaning and sheds light on the other. The problem is neither one nor the other, but problems arise when we favour one over the other, or fail to acknowledge what is involved in attempting to manage the difference. Then we experience both as polarized, rather than complementary. Marriage without romantic love – shared dreams, passion, some degree of spontaneous folly – can become a drudge. But at its best, it yields a satisfying companionship, a sense of fulfilment through sharing duty and honouring sincerely-made promises. Most importantly, it can provide the stability needed by children and adults alike to feel rooted in existence. Here is Tony Parsons, from his novel *Man and Boy*:

> You should never underestimate the power of the nuclear family. These days coming from an unbroken home is like having independent means, or Paul Newman's eyes, or a big cock. It's one of life's true blessings, given to just a lucky few.[5]

Such security is invaluable for children. But it is not all a bed of roses. The reality is that this security often comes at the cost of individual freedom and personal sacrifice, rather than through both partners' mutual empowerment and informed choices. Parsons continues:

> But those unbroken homes can lull you into a false sense of security. When I was growing up, I took it for granted that every marriage would be as stable and everlasting as my mum and dad's – including my own. My parents made it look easy. But it's not easy at all.[6]

The unerringly stable marriage, as Parsons tells us, though it offered a safe nest from which to be launched, could fail to teach its offspring how to manage the difficulties inherent in relationships. Perhaps the most important skill is learning how to manage difference and conflict. Once the prohibition against complaining – or having feelings in general – came to be lifted, these difficulties were experienced in spades.

There is a further difficulty with the kind of marriage that settles for stability at any price. Behind the sometimes desperate clinging to security, there may be a sense of unreality. Partners in this kind of marriage seem more like frightened children assuming parental roles than genuine grown ups. We will say more about partners acting from what we call 'parent mode' later on.

It is hardly surprising, therefore, that when the post-war generations, having benefited from increased material welfare and educational opportunities, as well as the stability which their parents' marriages provided, found themselves in an expanding world of information and personal choice, they swung firmly towards the polar opposite. In the main, their choice was for freedom, exploration and the expression of individuality. With the lid lifted, anything seemed better than replicating the patterns of parents who had never fully explored their options in the field of intimacy. In this climate, the value of having roots was easily lost when weighed against the personal sacrifices that seemed to accompany them. The old relationship style seemed to offer little juice in the sensuous new world and its stability was interpreted as shackles which could now be cut.

And what of the romantic ideal? Despite its eternal allure and ever-renewable box-office formula, the Hollywood version was also failing to convince. It was too stereotypical, too naïve and too transparent for the new worldly wise. For what was the outcome of this ideal? Follow any happy Hollywood ending to its conclusion and it would inevitably settle into the familiar routine. Wedding bells, 'happy families' – the same old trap.

What happened to the less critical who bought the ticket nevertheless and fell out of glorious love before they got to the happy ending or after the first round of family life? Often it was pain and disappointment, or premature exhaustion.

Searching for Love and Freedom

If neither security nor romantic ideals could offer a workable model for modern relationships, what alternatives were there? One answer that came bounding in during the late sixties, fired by utopian politics and mind-expanding drugs, was 'free love'.

This one appealed to the adventurous. No more slavery to romantic notions of undying love! Throw away the outdated gender roles and the restrictions of the family model with its resulting co-dependency! Let children be born from unions of love, however transitory! Abandon jealousy! Don't make your partner a possession! Let men be free to have feelings and women to be sexual beings! Enjoy it while it lasts and if it doesn't feel good, part on friendly terms and move on to better things. Don't hinder the fulfilment of your own potential nor stand in the way of the other finding themselves!

It's not hard to spot the attractions or to be moved by the beauty of the vision. Men and women as equals, free to enjoy sex and to explore the endless possibilities of love and desire; relationships without commitment or responsibility; the promise of excitement, fun, sex, freedom, individualism and constant choice; no guilt, no duty, no shame, no ties. It was fun for a while for some – particularly the males – but it was no guarantee of happiness, it provided zero stability and someone was usually left holding the baby.

Has all this freedom brought us closer to a healthier and happier society? We have more choices, more material comforts and more information than anybody could have imagined 50 years ago, but it is not certain that our quality of life has improved. In fact, people appear to be more alienated, more alone and more emotionally wary than ever. Although sexual freedom has become the norm for the young and people enter relationships far more sexually experienced than they used to, most of us still yearn for a long-term relationship, even if we do not know how to manage one. And here we run into a serious problem.

The normalization of freedom encourages us to enjoy it 'while it lasts', but serves to increase our feelings of failure and loneliness when we can't find or create the kind of relationship we want.

Despite our amazing feats of technical skill, we have not developed a matching facility for solving the riddle of human interaction. We have had a revolution in communication and information technology – we can speak to each other at any time of day, wherever we are – but what shall we say to each other? For at the same time there is a growing ignorance of how to maintain any satisfactory depth and fulfilment in personal and intimate relations. Despite an obsession with voyeuristic sexual imagery and the general philosophy that sex should be fun for all and forever, *en masse* we are still profoundly ignorant about physical love and sexual intimacy.

Partners still find it hard to talk openly about things that are important between them. For example, recently we came across a newspaper article that featured couples who don't have sex. This was presented as an apparent rarity. However, our experience as counsellors is that couples in relationship difficulties will be most unlikely to be having much sex, unless they are cut off from their own emotional and bodily realities. Here is a young woman interviewed about how she and her partner dealt with the problem:

> Sometimes I'd like to talk to him about it, but it's also totally understood that we don't talk about it. It would feel like a terrible intrusion.[7]

In our alienation we long to be reconnected with each other, but we do not know how. The effects of this disconnection are as vague as they are wide-ranging. Could it be that the explosion of the use of mobile telephones, the drug culture, the fashion world, the internet, are all sustained by our need to know we matter and our desire to feel connected? Perhaps, ultimately, the potential barrenness of our civilization – the exploitative commercialism, the depletion of natural resources, the pollution of the Earth – is fired by an inner drought, a deep thirst for feeling connected to others, body, heart and soul, in a way that only genuine intimacy can provide.

How can we benefit from the worthwhile achievements of our modern age without getting stuck in the tendency to opt for short-term gain?

From Crisis to Opportunity in Relationships

At the beginning of this chapter we suggested that crises can sometimes be 'reframed' as opportunities. If we approach the Western crisis in intimate relationships as if it were a 'phase we are going through' (as people used to say of their children when they had trouble understanding them) we may have a better chance of seeing the problem in context.

In fact, we suggest that it makes a lot of sense to see this crisis as part of an *adolescent phase of development* which the West has to negotiate. If we begin to think like this, we can acknowledge the importance of searching a new blueprint for intimate relationships.

Like adolescents, we are keen to experiment with models entirely different from those of our parents. But as adolescents contemplating sex, relationships and marriage we only seem to have two choices. First, we may take our adolescent experimentation to the extreme. The downside of this is that we may spend our lives searching for the eternal party, leaving the results of our promiscuity and irresponsibility for someone else to clean up.

On the other hand, the voice inside which says: 'Grow up, settle down and make the best of it!' is hardly attractive. This option is no longer convincing, for, as we have seen, it tends toward repression rather than freedom and encourages pseudo-adulthood rather than true adulthood. If we opt for this, we are likely to sabotage it through our impatience or resentment — by giving up as soon as it gets difficult, leaving home like an adolescent once more, leaving someone else to be the reluctant parent while we try it all over again with someone else.

But let us not simply dismiss this adolescent phase too soon. Until relatively recently, people were married off straight from puberty and usually died by the time they were 40. There was no adolescence to speak of. Adolescence is new. It wasn't until the phenomena of Elvis Presley and the Beatles had woken the big money merchants up to the fact that children could become consumers of recorded products that society began to take adolescence seriously. When the liberation of state-assisted divorce arrived in the late 1940s it meant that men and women had a better chance of following their feelings, their choices, their desire, their excitement and their dreams. All these are valuable qualities of the adolescent.

No, the problem is not adolescence, the problem is staying stuck in it.

Purpose for Freedom

We deserve our freedom; we have waited a long time for it. But a true freedom is not the rebellion of an adolescent. A *chosen* freedom includes awareness and responsibility. It is as if we have not been ready for freely chosen committed relationships. Adolescents cannot really handle them.

A parallel view was recently expressed on a television programme about the morality of adultery. Former Bishop John Shelby Spong, now a lecturer at Harvard, was explaining that the issue was not adultery but rather what it meant to be in a committed relationship, referred to on the programme as 'monogamy':

As far as I can see monogamy hasn't yet been practised. True monogamy takes an absolute equality between one man and one woman. Absolute equality – political, social and religious – every kind of equality. I think we will evolve into true monogamy where men and women are absolutely at one. But until our society is at the place where women and men are equal in every way we cannot have true monogamy, but a monogamous pattern only.[8]

Spong reminds us that we have been waiting for a time when male and female energies are in better balance. Previously, on the outer stage, the men have been overactive, while the women have been overpassive. As the power balance begins to shift we are ready for a new equality. Here is Spong again:

> True monogamy involves the deep interaction of people as equals, and that is what I favour. I really do believe that there is something absolutely wonderful about investing your life and your love in your partner who is equal in every way, and sharing every aspect of your life.[9]

We think he is absolutely right, but we see equality as only a beginning. Until we are free to choose *not to* engage in committed relationships we are not properly free to choose for them. If our intimate relationships are to *mature* we will have to assume equality as a prerequisite. We will require freedom, but not at the expense of depth. We will commit to our relationships, but will want them to take us a step further: into and *beyond* ourselves, and towards the other.

This is a transformative step which involves stalking the fiery soul of intimate relationships. We believe that falling in love is a message from the gods, from the soul. To follow this message to its source is a mysterious and challenging adventure in which we commit ourselves to be transformed. Exactly what that commitment and transformation entails is what we shall be exploring in this book.

We believe that it is worth viewing the current changes in relationships as a process, not an outcome, a process that may not even have reached its climax yet. Nevertheless, the dice have been thrown. The players are men and women, the rules are the forces of love and power, the balance of freedom and commitment. We believe that relationships can transform men and women who consciously engage in them. Avoiding the challenges of committed relationships may be a catastrophe, with which we may be gambling the lives of future generations; purposefully taking them up appears to have a complementary beneficent power.

We believe that there exists a dynamic potential – which up until now has been hidden from us – in the seemingly impossible alchemy between a man and a woman. We know that it is more than simply making babies. We know that reaching for this next step will demand awareness, courage and perseverance, as well as the ability to tolerate our own feelings. Perhaps humanity has not yet been ready for this secret. Perhaps we had to grow up first. Perhaps we had to leave home.

If we realize this potential, it could make a difference to everything.

CHAPTER 3

Falling in Love

I've got you under my skin,
I've got you deep in the heart of me,
So deep in my heart that you're really a part of me
I've got you under my skin

I've tried so not to give in
I said to myself 'This affair never will go so well'
But why should I try to resist when, darling, I know so well
That I've got you under my skin

I'd sacrifice anything come what might
For the sake of having you near,
In spite of a warning voice that comes in the night
And repeats, repeats in my ear:
'Don't you know little fool, you never can win.
Use your mentality! Wake up to reality!'
But each time I do
Just the thought of you
Makes me stop before I begin,
Because I've got you under my skin...

Cole Porter[1]

Can you remember when you first fell in love? Do you dare? Perhaps you're still in love with your partner? Maybe you didn't *fall* in love, you just sort of drifted together, moving from joint interests to joint address to joint accounts?

However you got there, you may have had some kind of vision of how the relationship would unfold. Perhaps this was very clear to you and openly shared between the two of you. But most likely you never really thought or talked about it. It just felt right and you both trusted that you wanted enough of the same things to make a go of it. Chances are that you did not have lawyers make out a contract between you, as some of the wealthy do today! Whatever your story, there is little doubt that you brought a whole array of longings, dreams, hopes and fears with you into the relationship while hardly aware of them.

In *Women who Run with the Wolves*, Clarissa Pinkola Estes describes the process of falling in love by means of a story about the adventures of an absent-minded fisherman. We think that we need metaphors to talk about love and that fishing is an apt one. So we will borrow hers for a moment.

We would like to invite you to come with us on a fishing trip. Let us say that you have a little boat and you are drifting around with your line hanging over the side. Just imagine that instant when, after ages of waiting and thinking about nothing, you feel a tug from the deep on the end of your line. Imagine the rush of adrenaline, the excitement of catching something, the thrill of not knowing what will emerge from the water... The fish or lover – let's call it your 'catch' – could be anything ... everything ... or nothing. Whatever it is, it has certainly caught your attention. It is something unknown, with the power to fire your imagination and stir your slumbering hopes and dreams. What until now may have been a half-hearted way of passing the time suddenly brings you into the present moment, with all your senses alert.

What was it like when you first met your 'other half'? What sort of a catch were they? What did you notice about them? What made this particular person stand out from the crowd? What spurred you on in the pursuit to get to know them better? Was it a certain look in their eye, the way they walked or something in their tone of their voice? Maybe they just looked great to you – beautifully dressed, sweet, confident... Perhaps you had sex on your first meeting and something was different about it. Or maybe it was a meeting of equal minds, perhaps you engaged in stimulating exchanges and felt that finally here was a person who understood your way of thinking and shared your worldview.

Some fall in love ecstatically, some are driven to distraction, some drift towards each other, others simply feel comfortable with one another. Whichever way it happened for you, it cannot be explained rationally. You may find that you remember it as if it were yesterday and know exactly what the attraction was, or you may find it impossible to remember or to pinpoint anything in particular. Yet whatever it was that caught your attention, you also were caught. For we are both the fisherman and the catch.

The first encounter with the unknown other is full of potential and unspoken promise, and something extraordinary happens. Lovers experience a complete turnaround in their personalities and behaviour. Suddenly everything runs at a heightened intensity. Do you remember the time before knowing whether your feelings were reciprocated? Can you recall the swings between the excitement of daring to believe and the fear of possible rejection and disappointment? Do you remember the gentle feeling of joy in the pit of your stomach at the thought of the next phone call? And how the same joy could turn to despair – or cool self-sufficiency – when the phone didn't ring, only to evaporate into the dizzy air the next time you answered and there they were, wanting to see if you were free? Or, if you were the one making the call, you could probably tell a story about how many times you picked up the phone, just to put it back again, not wanting to seem too eager or too pushy, playing it cool in case your advances were unwelcome. When we are in love we experience more emotion than ever before – and perhaps those whose love is unrequited experience most of all.

Then somehow it happens: the new lovers manage to communicate their feelings for each other. They begin to declare themselves. Sometimes they become tremendously expressive. They write poems late at night. There is a feeling of exquisite harmony in the air. The splendour of surrendering and melting into the shared dreams and joint visions merges with the smells and sounds and sensations of the new intimate pleasures. Do you remember how the energy rushed through you, sweet and calm, yet powerful as a torrential river? Being in love can be a somewhat ungrounding experience. The moon can become important. Some people go a little crazy, fall in love with the whole world, see no limits, do rash things. Perhaps in love with love itself, they perform senseless acts of beauty. Sometimes they forget to eat.

When we are in love and that love is returned we feel alive, whole, beautiful, complete. There's a naturalness to it. We are suffused with soul. Our deepest longings are simultaneously stirred *and* met, and the result is a feeling of profound connectedness. Perhaps when you met your partner your whole life felt different. Whatever you were doing, wherever you were, the very thought of the other made you feel warm and good. You looked different, walked taller, spoke more confidently or calmly. Colours were brighter, music sweeter. The whole imperfect world slotted into place, and you with it.

And the other was with you all the time, even if you were miles apart. Just as in that old Cole Porter song, when we are in love we carry the imprint of that one special person right under our skin, right next to our heart, as a part of us, almost closer than we are to ourselves.

What Were You Hoping to Catch?

While he is waiting to get a bite our fisherman keeps company with his daydreams. This is an apt metaphor for how we go about the business of everyday life, barely conscious of our fantasies about how life would be if we met that special person. Mostly we just drift about with our lines hanging loose, with vague notions of what we want to catch, busy with how good we'll feel when we bring it home.

So when the hook goes in and we feel the tug on the line, we are already convinced that this is it – the real thing, the dream come true. And it certainly feels like that to begin with.

The first major change is that we begin to enjoy being who we are. Whether being in love brings out our truest nature or whether we simply are on our best behaviour is hard to say. Maybe the two are connected. But it is clear that during this period we are able to rise above the more disagreeable aspects which normally lurk around the edges of our character. It is as if in the presence of the magical beloved our ugly parts simply vanish. Perhaps this is what gives rise to the saying 'Love conquers all'.

All is well until that moment when we first catch a glimpse of a different side to our beloved. At first we don't pay much attention to it. It can even endear them to us. Isn't this what it is all is about – learning to love the other with all their imperfections? It feels good to be the person who can do that and we all long to bring out the goodness in ourselves. So now we not only feel loved and wanted, we also experience ourselves as loving. We have done it. The sails are set, the breeze is warm, the fish are jumping and the sun is on the horizon.

But there is just one cloud. At a certain moment the 'warning voice that comes in the night' starts to whisper faintly: 'But you ain't seen nothing yet!' The first moment of disquiet will not go away. Do you remember the first time you knew there was more

35

to your lover than met the eye and chose to ignore it? A woman told us once how that happened on her wedding day.

We left the church to the cheering of our friends and family and walked towards the car waiting to carry us to the reception. My newly wedded husband proceeded to enter the car before me, leaving me to gather my dress and awkwardly climb in after him. He never noticed anything and carried on waving and smiling to our guests as if nothing had happened. And to him, nothing had. But in a split second I had a multitude of thoughts and feelings flashing through me. I was shocked, hurt and angry. Tears rose up in my eyes. It happened so fast that I didn't even stop in my movements.

As I took my place next to my husband, he turned and smiled lovingly at me and a similar flash happened. This time I explained it all to myself. I had never expected him to keep doors open for me: I was fit and healthy and climbing into a car posed no problem whatsoever. He was probably excited and relieved that it had all gone well — maybe preoccupied about the speech he had to make later on. I even managed to reassure myself that nobody would find tears in a bride's eyes strange.

It all happened so fast that I hardly had time to consciously register it. All my husband saw was his bride smiling back at him with tears of happiness in her eyes. We had a wonderful reception and I soon forgot the episode. And yet, as you can see, it left a lasting and uncannily detailed impression behind.

For a fleeting moment, the veil had been lifted. But years of married life would pass before the memory would return to her consciousness to yield a deeper meaning.

The reasons for not paying more attention to such feelings in the initial stages are both simple and extremely complex. The complexity has to do with the fact that we are all unaware of what really underlies our initial attraction to each other. Even a fair amount of psychological knowledge provides little guarantee of any useful awareness. For falling in love bypasses the rational process. It stirs something from the deep and we are invited to a different level of adventure – one in which we have little control. In modern France, the law continues to make allowances for acts which are perpetrated under the influence of being in love – *le crime passionnel*.

The simple explanation is not easy, either. It is simply that we have to be fully caught: hook, line and sinker. This kind of simplicity is more like innocence. It is more like the archetypal quality of simplicity attributed to the Fool in the Tarot who stands on the top of a precipice. Falling in love involves a daring leap made from a truly innocent part within us. It cannot be done either rationally or consciously. Innocence is required to allow fools to rush in where angels fear to tread.

And here is the beauty of falling in love: we become the trusting fool and, forgetting ourselves, step off the cliff and are held, mysteriously, in mid-air for a blessed second. We fall out of our ordinary roles and identifications. Naturally, we don't waste time thinking about *why* we feel so good when we are with our special one. We get on and enjoy it. Besides, there seems to be an in-built mechanism to this process which ensures just that: when we are in love, whatever aspects of our lives usually haunt us now give us respite, for the simple reason that these parts are currently perfectly satisfied.The ordinary becomes extraordinary. We can relax and enjoy the feeling of completeness in our being.

It was half past six on a Friday evening. The London Underground was as busy as it could be. There were people everywhere, swarming like ants, purposely making their way up and down the moving staircases, running for trains, heaving bags and briefcases through the ticket machines. The cold wind whistling through the station seemed to increase the pressure to get on and get home.

But he didn't care. He stood at the bottom of the escalator as if transfixed, listening to a busker with a strange intensity. It was an old love song, one he had heard many times before, but he had never heard *it until tonight, until this moment. His eyes were moist and shining. He was unaware of the crowds and the people trying to get past him.*

'Yes!' he shouted, not caring if anyone heard him. 'That's exactly it!'

He swung her round on his arm triumphantly and, gliding over the cement floor as one, they finally took their place on the crowded escalator, pressing close together, aware of each other's bodies even through their thick winter coats.

'How can people hear such a song and just keep moving?' he asked her, not expecting an answer.

She squeezed his hand. 'You oaf,' she said tenderly, looking deeply into his eyes and smiling that smile, the one that could envelop the world.

She loved this crazy enthusiastic side of him. When they were together like this, even grimy old London seemed like gay Paris – it didn't matter where they were, she just felt glad to be alive. Even when they were apart she would catch herself feeling a warm glow, as if she were somehow fully whole, complete, both excited yet profoundly calm. Sometimes she would be so absorbed in this feeling that someone in the office could be talking to her and she would completely ignore them. But when she turned round and noticed them she would smile that smile and they would forgive her.

These days she seemed to exude love, and it was infectious.

That Certain Something

Have you ever thought about why you fell in love precisely with *your* partner and not somebody else? And why it is that the person who has the ability to catapult your best friend's mind into orbit, alter their heart rate (and start other body parts throbbing in expectation) leaves you rather cool, though you find them perfectly nice? Similarly, the person who performs this magic on you has no effect on your friend. It's curious, isn't it?

Of course, we may have our individual preferences for certain types. Some prefer blondes, others brunettes. Some like it hot, others not. The woman who looks too heavy to one man appears irresistibly voluptuous to another. A man who is casually dressed and not over-groomed looks deliciously rough and manly to one woman, yet is an offputting scruff-bag to another. There are thousands of beautiful voluptuous women and as many delicious male scruffs in the world. Would any one of them do? If so, what's all the fuss about when a relationship breaks up? Go catch another one, there are plenty of fish in the sea!

But of course it isn't just down to appearances. What people call 'personality' comes into it. And mannerisms, and a combination of things not so easily defined. We have to go deeper than this. If we start to reflect on just *what* caught our attention and what was attractive enough to result in the relationship we now find ourselves in, we often find something quite perverse. It turns out to be that what was most attractive about the partner is also most charged with ambivalence.

This is a complex idea so we will try to illustrate it. In our story, Nick still remembers how at the beginning he found it new and interesting that Helena was able to say 'no' to him, to disagree with and challenge him. He liked this assertive side of her. At first! Helena has never forgotten how moved and fascinated she was the first time she spent a whole evening listening to Nick talk about himself, his life and his ideas. This was not a one-syllable man! He really talked and shared his feelings. But, as we revealed at the beginning of the book, the enchantment soon wore off. Would he ever be interested in her, Helena sometimes silently wondered.

We will explore later what causes the qualities that are initially attractive to come to be seen in a very different light. But for now, we suggest that what is so right about the match is the accuracy with which the partner can put us in touch with parts of our being which have been lost to our memory. Until now, these missing parts have remained fully alive, but unstirred, in the depths of our being, at an almost cellular level, until that certain person is found. And that is probably why we have to catch someone just right for us.

For example, in the story of the newly-weds, what interests us is not whether the husband behaved rightly or wrongly – it was their wedding day and we can readily understand that he was nervous and she got upset. What suggests that something deeper was at play is how the wife was affected – the force with which these feelings hit her. Her shocked state seems out of proportion to the event, even to her. She neither shared the incident with her husband, nor even remembered it until years later during a heated argument. Then, as much to her own surprise as to her husband's total bewilderment, she heard herself recounting the incident in order to conclusively prove that he was no different from his misogynist father. It wasn't until she gave birth to their first child, a boy, that she learned from her mother how her father had been disappointed when his first-born turned out to be a girl. Then she understood something about her initial attraction to her husband and her strong reactions to the incident at their wedding, where he failed to honour her femininity.

Once Bitten, Twice Shy

What if there was no ethereal music or flights of fancy into altered states of (un)consciousness when you met your partner, but instead good solid ground, perhaps supported by friendship or maybe a mutual appreciation of the pleasures of music or sex? You entered the relationship sober and awake, rather than in an ecstatic, quasi-psychotic state. Does that mean that you had no dreams or longings?

For old-timers in the arena of love, the first reaction is likely to be more cautious. And yet, even underneath the dampener of experience, the same hopes and fears are awakened. But the scars of love are slow to heal and can produce an automatic tendency to armour the heart against being hurt again. So when love knocks on our door, we don't recognize it. Having learned not to trust it, we greet it with suspicion and either ignore it or rationalize it.

Here are the words of a man, quoted in a national newspaper, who, a year after separating from his wife of 16 years and their two children, finds himself tentatively putting the line out again:

> I'm now four months into a new relationship. She's going through a separation herself, and I can help in a practical sense. I don't expect it to last. She'll probably go back to her husband. Our relationship is very different from my marriage, quite unconditional. I get a kick out of giving; I don't want anything back. It's rewarding and fulfilling, but if the relationship ends, I'll cope.[2]

This is a complex statement. To us, he reveals himself as a man who has not yet come to terms with the ending of his marriage. We may speculate that what he calls 'unconditional' love without attachment to the outcome could be a rationalization of his detached and wary resignation. Likewise, his practical helping and giving may cover a need to feel in control of a situation that could otherwise render him unbearably vulnerable. The 'warning voice that comes in the night' might be saying: 'If you're only superficially involved you can't get hurt.' Now what would happen if this new woman actually *did* commit to being with him?

The resistance to commit to love can sometimes be understood as an attempt to protect against a premature knowledge of the pain of falling out of love. Now that marriage and commitment are no longer the only acceptable ways to follow on from falling in love, lovers are exposed to powerful emotional and psychological forces without any structure to hold them. Nor are they supplied with any new knowledge to contexualize their experiences. So the pain can be too much to face; the resistance is understandable. But there is a problem with this stance. If you already believe love can't last, you make yourself wise before the event and you lose your innocence. If you don't fall like an innocent fool, if you're too closed down and scared of getting hurt, you may have no chance to go beyond disappointment and out the other side. You need the fool's energy to progress. But if you are not held within the structure of a committed relationship the forces will be too much, even for the fool. They will eat you up when you fall out of love.

And that's where we must turn to next.

But first, a small diversion.

A Short History of Falling in Love

The reader may be tempted to imagine that the universal belief in the idea of falling in love is normal, natural and as old as the hills. A cursory glance at any bestselling novel display at an airport or through the women's magazines at the news-stand or the reviews of new movies in the entertainment guide would support such a view. But although men and women have undoubtedly relished romance and sex throughout the ages, the concept of freely chosen love as the basis for a shared life is a relatively new one.

In many parts of the world marriages continue to be arranged by the parents of the couple and are regarded as a social event and a financial agreement within a clan or an extended family network. In many cases, the bride is still more like a possession, given by her family as a token of solidarity to her husband's family. She may sometimes be bought, but more often she brings a dowry with her. In ancient India this would have been a certain number of cows; these days it is Rupees. In village India today the material benefits of a match are primary, though just to make sure, the local astrologer is always consulted on the subject of both the marriage and the wedding day.

In rural Greece a dowry can still be a bridal chest, full of weavings. Here is a true story from Greece, where the new and the old worlds, East and West, are still talking to each other. The setting is the late 1970s.

> There was a certain unmarried woman on the island of Evvia who was the finest weaver in the district. But she was far from what was considered an eligible bride, due to her looks and the origins of her family. It was imagined that she might never marry. In awe, the locals would whisper about her bridal chest, for she was still actively weaving at the age of 40. This chest continued to swell with amazing treasures, which would probably remain unseen until her death.

The negotiations around marriages and the attempts of young lovers to foil the arrangements of their elders have been the subject of countless stories in which love attempts to transcend the economic or political designs of the match. In our Western tradition we recall Tristan and Isolde or Romeo and Juliet; the fight for Helen of Troy was the major myth of the ancient European world. Many of these stories displayed a star-crossed destiny which would give way to tragedy. Thus the idea of romantic love seems to have built in a certain tendency towards disappointment, or unfulfilment. As Shakespeare, in his master-piece on the irrational forces, *A Midsummer Night's Dream*, tells us:

> Ay me! For aught that I could ever read,
> Could ever hear by tale or history,
> The course of true love never runs smooth.

It was in Western Europe that the notion of falling in love really took root. Eventually, as in so many other areas, the rest of the world had to keep pace. Is this the West's special gift to the world? Or an attempt to balance out the excessive rationality that Western civilization stands for now? We cannot tell, but we may speculate on its origins of the worship of romantic love, tracing it to the mediaeval cult of the Troubadours and the Romancers of Provence. Here love – or *Amor* – was raised to a high art-form, almost a religion, in which the fulfilment and consumption of a love between a man and a woman was far less important than their ethereal connection and mutual dedica-tion. The culture flourished widely but briefly, seeming to provide an answer to some of the difficulties personal erotic love posed to the dominant religion of the era.

Love was a big problem for the Christian Church. How could you embrace the concept of couplehood, which needed sexual attraction to hold it together, when sexuality was regarded as the root of 'original sin'? Marriage was said to be OK for the masses, but how might the ordinary couple conduct their union when the model couple had a miraculous virgin birth as its outcome? And then there was the subject of women. Here the authorities were in serious trouble as a result of not being able to properly answer the first two questions. Consequently, a woman's sexual desire came to be seen as a sign of demonic pos-session. The man who followed his instincts had 'succumbed' to her bewitching powers. And if unbridled loving passion, rape or visits to prostitutes were all the same sin, why respect your wife?

Pagan antiquity seemed on surer ground here than dogmatic Christianity. And, perhaps unsurprisingly, in matters of sex and love, European country folk tentatively adhered to the vestiges of ancient lore for many a year. The old mythological world was rooted in nature, with its never-ending round of fertilization and fruition, death and new life. The great god of fertilization, Pan, was also the god of lovers. He signified big trouble to the Church and so was reinvented as the horned goat-bearded Satan, ready to catch out any sinner. Knowledge of his beneficial powers was driven underground, sometimes literally. To this day you may see his effigy in caves in parts of Western Europe, if you ask the right people to show you. So the concept of a loving erotic union between men and women had a forbidden, underground nature imposed upon it.

And there was a further difficulty. The irrational quality which accompanies falling in love implies great risk, a personal surrender, a deep vulnerability, due not only (we would add) to the sexuality inherent in it, but also to the unconscious processes or powers which take over. These powers are human, or at least more like 'gods' than the powers of a Heavenly Father. In their daily life, which was centred on the cycles of agriculture, country people continued to involve these powers by means of certain rituals and traditions which had persisted, or been partly remembered, from ancient times. Often they were convened at the time of the ancient pagan fertility rites – the May Day festival with its May Queen and dancing around the pole. According to Oxford historian Sir James Frazer, in some communities the time of planting had involved obligatory 'unbridled sensuality between men and their wives',[3] while in others the sowers stayed away from their partners so as to conserve the concentration of their fertile energy.

Other customs grew up around the harvest festivals, when the fruition of fertility could not be ignored. Such occasions invariably featured the entire community, due to the work involved. They gave young men and women an opportunity to fraternize against a backdrop of communal labour, followed by feasting, drinking and dancing. The rites of Bacchus would frequently invoke Aphrodite. In our great great-grandparents' day many of these customs were still just alive, something to which many of the novels of Thomas Hardy attest. In other places they may have held on for longer. In the Perigord region of south-west France, for example, as recently as the 1930s there was custom of courtship which went on in a secret but well-known fashion. Jean-Luc Toussaint describes how shelling the ripened walnuts would be the task of the women, and a passing suitor:

> could signal his interest in a girl by slipping a tiny, round walnut ... called a *cacalou* ... into her shelling tray. What the little nut lacked in market value it made up for in romantic significance.[4]

For the urban population it was the poets and novelists of the nineteenth century who repopularized the fashion for romantic love, but it was not until the twentieth was well underway that the idea began to become universal. Tin Pan Alley and Hollywood ensured that the romantic dream was established for the masses. How many songs and stories deal with the subject of love? But the age of mass disillusionment was soon to follow, for how could real life match the glamorous version portrayed on the silver screen? How could the mundanity of everyday life come up to the standard set by the great romantic ideal?

The West had fallen deeply in love with love itself – and was bound to fall out, sooner or later.

CHAPTER 4

Dancing in the Dark

You never close your eyes anymore when I kiss your lips,

There's no tenderness like before in your fingertips,

You're trying hard not to show it, Baby,

But Baby ... [perumpa tum tum!] ... Baby, I know it!

You've lost that lovin' feelin',

Wo-o, that lovin' feelin',

You've lost that lovin' feelin',

Now it's gone, gone, gone, wo-o-o-o...

Now there's no welcome look in your eyes when I reach for you,

And now you're starting to criticize little things I do.

It makes me just feel like crying, Baby,

'Cos Baby, something beautiful's dying

You've lost that lovin' feelin',

Wo-o, that lovin' feelin',

You've lost that lovin' feelin',

Now it's gone, gone, gone,

And I can't go on ... anymore...

Wo-o-o-o...

Barry Mann, Cynthia Weil and Phil Spector[1]

Oh dear. How we loved that song in the late sixties. How we identified with it. How many pangs of collapsing love were eulogized by the deep male voices of the Righteous Brothers. Even if they felt righteously sorry for themselves, we knew what they meant. And we loved it.

For the song gets the first feelings of falling out of love exactly right. The crisis is the loss of 'that lovin' feelin' '. It's not the singers' fault, everything is attributed to the partner, here called 'Baby'. But the song is also faintly ridiculous and now we chuckle as we sense how even the brothers' serious deep voices fail to conceal that what is lost is not love, but the singers' feeling of *being* loved, entirely and completely. Unconditional love is disappearing fast and in this song the boys feel sorry for themselves – as boys will. 'Wo-o-o.'

However, let us not be too quick to dismiss it. There is something else very strange in the form of this song – the music. It is not really in a rock or pop idiom, it is far more theatrical, more like a musical. The music gives us the idea that this is the beginning of a great drama. It is the kind of song which might have opened a popular musical, in the tradition of *There's No Business Like Show Business*. And in our relationship story that feeling is just about right, for an archetypal drama is unfolding and it is all beyond our control. With the loss of the fantasy of unconditional love the relationship starts to grow up – but it's a painful start and we will be inclined to fight it all the way.

Falling out of Love

Subonfu Somé is an African woman who had her marriage arranged for her by the elders of her tribe in Burkino Faso and was then sent to the West to live with her husband in order to teach what the fast disappearing indigenous world might have to offer. Nothing is more different, she says, than the concept of relationships in the West and in her native village. For a start, in the village a relationship is not private — *everyone* gets involved. It is in everyone's interest that each relationship becomes a success. But most importantly, Subonfu reckons that in the West we have an inflated way of beginning our pair-bonding. She says that here relationships start at the very top — and then they can only fall, because there is nowhere else to go:

> Since a relationship must grow, and must be constantly in motion, and it's already at the top, where is it going to go? It's going to go down.[2]

We agree, for we see relationships as a developmental process and falling out of love as the real starting-point. If this notion is right, then disappointment is the royal road to waking up from a dream: it can lead us to deepen our awareness of ourselves and our ability to be intimate. Disappointment has the power to sharpen the mind amazingly. The famous Tibetan teacher Chögyam Trungpa Rinpoche once said that there was nothing so clear as disappointment:

> Disappointment is a good sign of basic intelligence. It cannot be compared to anything else: it is so precise, obvious and direct. It is the best chariot to use on the path of Truth.[3]

But this is all very well after the event. When you are *in* the disappointment it is extremely unpleasant. And perhaps you don't see yourself as being 'on the path of Truth' — you are simply trying to manage a relationship and get on with your life!

If falling in love is like climbing to the top of a hill, then falling out of love is like falling off. It's bound to be scary and it hurts. It is a huge adventure now threatening to get out of control. Falling in love involves the most powerful spiritual force in the universe — *love* — and the most powerful physical one – *attraction*. Everything on the planet is held in place by gravity, the application of the Earth's attractive power. But attraction has its twin and science suggests that it was the opposite magnetic force – *repulsion* – that began the creation of the universe in the 'Big Bang'.

Moving to the Land of 'If Only'

In an intimate relationship we can move from attraction to repulsion very fast. It scares the heck out of us and we retreat, thinking or yelling how unfair it all is: 'You've lost that lovin' feelin'...' 'You're not who I thought you were...' Then we begin to reason: 'This is not how I wanted us to turn out...' 'If this is what we do to each other, we can't be right for each other...'

This is the voice of disappointment. There is no mistaking it. When we finally face the loss of attraction, the loss of the good feelings, even if it happens very gradually over some years, it is a personal catastrophe. Sometimes we put it to the back of our minds and try to forget it, but it does not go away. Eventually we cannot deny it. It stares us in the face: 'This relationship is not working anymore.'

The first impulse is to want it to return to the way it was. In *Man and Boy*, Tony Parsons describes it brilliantly. After his hero has had a fling with a girl in the office, his betrayed wife Gina screams:

'It can't always be a honeymoon, you know.'

'I know, I know,' I said, but deep down inside what I thought was – *why not? why not?*

'We've been together for years. We have a child together. It can never be that Romeo and Juliet crap again.'

'I understand all that,' I said, and most of me really did. But a tiny, tiny part of me wanted to say – *Oh I'm off then*. Gina was right – I wanted us to be the way we were at the start. I wanted us to be like that forever.[4]

Men in particular seem to have a hankering for the glorious heady days of The Beginning. But relationships, like everything else in life, never go backwards. Once nudged out of peaceful sleep, they can only stagnate, go forwards or end. When it seems that the carpet has been pulled out from under our feet, or that we have been dumped on an emotional roller-coaster, we panic, and a part of us wants out immediately. This way we attempt to preserve in aspic what was rather than witness its painful demolition. It's perfectly understandable.

Baby, Baby, I'll get down on my knees to you,
If you would only love me like you used to do...
Bring back that lovin' feelin',
Wo-o, that lovin' feelin'...
'Cos it's gone, gone, gone...
And I can't go on, wo-o-o-o...

But there is no going back.

The sound of the Hoover in the other room mingled in his ears with the buzzing of a big fat bluebottle that seemed to be caught in the paper lampshade. 'This is perfect,' he thought to himself, 'the sound of utter exasperation.'

It was a warm Saturday morning and he wished he were playing tennis. But he had stayed at home because she had said why couldn't they spend a bit more time together at weekends. Now, on this lovely morning, how was she spending it? She was cleaning – again!

He had decided to use the moment to clear the desk and pay some of the bills that were beginning to mount up. But he could only find one or two of them and he knew there were more somewhere. A month ago he had brought home a couple of lovely aluminium-coloured filing baskets which he had found in that giant Swedish furniture store. They were just right for organizing the home paperwork: an in-tray and an out-tray. But she had refused to entertain the idea. 'Why are you so keen to make our home look like an office?' she had complained. 'Don't you get enough office life at work?'

He found the bills on the occasional table, still in their envelopes. Why did she – who was so intelligent and so efficient at her work – always put letters back in their envelopes, he wondered? It was so irritating.

When they first met he had loved the fact that she couldn't give a fig about the daily mechanics of life. She had always been interested in what it all meant, what lay behind things and what life was all about. It was so exciting being around her, it had changed everything. But these days he found that the way she could let the paperwork go to hell while at the same time cleaning like a woman possessed both baffling and deeply irritating.

She unplugged the Hoover, jammed her foot onto the cable release and watched the electric snake fly back into its lair. 'Thank God,' she sighed, 'that's over.' She stretched and heard him shuffling around in the next room. How was it that he could totally ignore the dirt, she wondered, and leave it all up to her?

In the beginning she had been delighted when he had said they could live anywhere, on any money, just as long as they were together. All he needed in a home was her (he obviously forgot to mention the television). But she had felt so important to him that nothing else mattered. But lately she had realized that domestically he was a total slob. Nothing else seemed to matter to him except what he thought important. He would be obsessive about his damned paperwork, but leave his rotten socks all over the place.

And she liked a clean house to relax in. She was fed up with playing mother and a housemaid. After all, it was the late nineties and women were meant to be emancipated now, and men sensitive.

'Oh well,' she thought as she put the Hoover back under the stairs, 'best not make a fuss. We've got the whole weekend ahead of us.' As she walked through the doorway, she resolved to greet him cheerfully and make the best of things.

'Isn't it gorgeous?' she said brightly. 'What shall we do today?'

'Well, the morning's nearly over,' he whined.

Instantly she braced herself as she felt her stomach pulling into a knot.

'God,' she groaned and turned on her heel.

You've Lost That Lovin' Feelin'

In many relationships, the first signs of disquiet usually appear after things have settled down a bit. Most couples begin to come down to earth after moving in together. Then life becomes more domestic than ethereal. In the past this would have been when the courting was over and marriage began. There is an old saying that love makes you blind and marriage makes you see again. Why should this be so?

Perhaps when we take on domestic roles we find ourselves acting more like parents than the free-spirited innocent children we felt like when we were deeply in love and on the loose. Sometimes one partner seems to transfer their affection to their work and the other to their babies. They are still in love, just not with each other. Or perhaps it is just that we start out presenting the best sides of ourselves, and with everything to gain, we rise to our best. While we enjoy the wholeness that the other partner conveys, it feels good. But after a while something happens. Do we start to feel safe and therefore stop trying so hard? Is it that when we are once more in a family we regress to a childish state? Do we resent the other for having stolen our freedom and then turn against them?

Whatever the reason, there seems to be a recognizable phase

in which the magic stops working. Dr Ellen J. Clephane, an American clinician, puts it like this:

> Falling in love is that magical beginning of a relationship in which our hearts stay almost continuously open. We exist for a time in the ecstasy of the love that we are, for which we give most of the credit to our beloved. Gradually, patterns of thought, emotion and behaviour from the past rise up and our hearts begin to close, for which most blame goes to the beloved.[5]

This is an important point. If we credit the lover for the working of the spell, then we automatically blame them when it fails. Criticism and irritation with the other begin. It is not that the other starts to exhibit little habits that you hadn't bargained for – like cutting toenails in bed – though it may be that too. No, more often than not, it seems to be specifically linked to those aspects of the other which formed part of the initial attraction.

As an outsider one is able to notice the precision with which falling out of love happens. But when you are in it, it feels bewildering and lonely. Both of you believe you have done your best to foster an environment in which love can grow. Both of you are equally devastated at being misunderstood, time and time again, by the person closest to you. This is when you need your friends. It's a good time to have a prolonged moan about your partner. If you are a woman, the chances are that any of your female friends will sympathize. At some stage in their lives they will probably have been in a similar situation, so getting together to vent your feelings is invaluable. Likewise, if you are a man, you will find yourself easily understood by your male friends, although you may have different ways of supporting each other.

But beware! The good friend must be more than a good listener. At this point it's not always helpful to have your friends buy the version of your partner that you wish to sell. It can prove more useful if they can empathize with your feelings and yet challenge you a little. And the reason is that something very specific is happening.

Falling in love is buying a ticket on the soul's roller-coaster. But falling out of love is an integral part of the ride if you want to savour the experience to its fullness.

'And Now You Start to Criticize the Little Things I Do'

The predictability of the attraction-irritation connection is too fascinating to ignore. We said earlier that the initial attraction was accompanied by some ambivalence. It is not until you fall out of love, however, that you start to experience this fully.

Let us imagine your partner as someone possessing various qualities which you admired over and above how physically attractive you found them. Perhaps they seemed 'socially at ease' or 'challenging' or maybe 'adventurous'. You could have noticed a sensitivity and empathy that warmed you or a sense of security which promised reliability. Maybe they were just different from the people you usually met and you were intrigued. When you 'locked on' to this person, like two modules meeting in outer space, you felt good precisely because they possessed the qualities which you craved. You felt whole and complete with them.

But after a while you started to get used to them and to revert to the old 'you' that you had always been. So now, when you see that your partner is able to operate *only* in the previously favoured mode, it starts to irk a little. The secure and reliable person now appears boring and predictable. The person who seemed so at ease socially now embarrasses you with their shallowness, while the adventurous challenger seems loud and intrusive. Where you were once intrigued, you are now irritated by this person who is simply so different from you that

55

you can't figure out why you were attracted to them in the first place. Whatever the quality you liked about them was, it now feels like a burden.

And before there's a chance to think this through, something else happens. You may notice that you respond to this part of the other in rather a similar way to how your mother or father responded to you (even though you swore that you would never turn out like them). Or, if you are beginning to have arguments, then perhaps your partner has already been accusing you of this very fact. You will quite naturally have denied it and referred the mistaken person back to their own behaviour (of course). But a vague worry does not go away.

To make matters worse, you realize that your partner has developed some alarming habits or attitudes which remind you of dear old mum or dad. When you met, you were convinced that they were absolutely nothing like them. In fact you were probably on the lookout for the polar opposite anyway. It can be something that seems quite minor, for example, their attitude to animals or to authorities. But it does irritate you. If you were attracted to someone who was just like one of your parents, you now start to remember what it was like when you felt you had to get out of the home.

Perhaps you notice that the ways in which decisions are now being made about what you both do, or what you purchase, have a familiar ring to them. If there are children around, you may notice that there are certain patterns of favouritism or tendencies to make alliances developing, and you don't like them. These things are too difficult to get your head around, but you may catch yourself wondering whether you have been through this before somewhere.

In different ways you are growing distant to one another. You may be reconsidering whether getting together was a good idea after all. Because this is *not* the person you bargained for. You may be wondering whether a committed relationship is right for you. There are some people for whom it just is not suited, right? Or at least not with *this* individual.

What has happened is that you have fallen out of love and into polarization.

PART 2

The Dance in the Dark

CHAPTER 5

When You Think It's All Over, It May Have Only Just Begun

Someone dancing inside us
learned only a few steps:
the 'Do-Your-Work' in 4/4 time,
the 'What-Do-You-Expect' waltz.
He hasn't noticed yet the woman
standing away from the lamp,
the one with the black eyes
who knows the rhumba,
and strange steps in jumpy rhythms
from the mountains in Bulgaria.
If they dance together,
something unexpected will happen.
If they don't, the next world
will be a lot like this one.

Bill Holm[1]

So, once partners have had a closer look at the catch hauled up from the depths of the sea of love, a new phase begins. This stage is characterized by disquiet, misgiving and sometimes shock. The energy between partners switches around and starts to move in opposite directions. Attraction turns into repulsion and, to a greater or lesser degree, couples begin to polarize. Where once they shared a world where all seemed to be one, now all is divided. Pleasant merger has given way to awkward separation. Is this because things have gone wrong or could it be that a deeper process is at work?

Let us for a moment take a look through the lens of developmental psychology. From this point of view, the shift seems to resemble the early phases of a child's psychological growth, where identity and consciousness begin to develop only by differentiating from, and thereby apparently losing, the original symbiosis with the mother. It is a necessary stage, but it involves a wrench from the known. Similarly, the arrival of this stage of a relationship signifies that it has entered a phase of *growth*, even if the partners feel that it's dying. A relationship is a dynamic living organism and it needs to grow. Energetically, the first move is from a position of pleasant and apparently agreed upon stability, which we call 'the stage of maintenance', to a stage of unexpected dynamism, which we call 'polarization'.

When people polarize they experience themselves as separate, different and often antagonistic towards each other. Sometimes it can be hard for them to say 'we' – they find it easier to say 'you', often with blame attached. This domestic polarization is not so different from that which we see everywhere on the wider stage of world politics. Racism, different ideologies and the concept of 'rogue states' keep nations polarized and, like the polarities on a battery, such forces can create a great deal of energy.

It can be difficult to co-exist with someone we think is wrong, selfish or misguided. Nevertheless, the energy generated by the polarization has an added function, we think. Without the precise difference that exists between male and female, no Third Being can be born. Polarization is a precursor to a new event, one which results in the willing coming together of the two polarized elements, both physically and psychologically. We call this phase 'alchemy'. We believe that there is a purpose to a couple coming apart, as if they have to build up sufficient charge for the potential growth of the relationship.

But while caught up in polarization, it is very difficult to feel any sense of a positive outcome. When couples are impelled only by the urge to return to the status quo or to separate, any suggestion of a creative alchemy or any new harmony exists only in the realms of speculation.

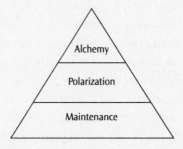

When a relationship is in polarization it is impossible to determine *where* it is going, but we can say something about *how* couples polarize. We think that couples are involved in bringing to term a great adventure: that of trying to live together as men and women, of becoming a unity where once they were fused individuals, of engaging in partnership and compromise without sacrifice or domination. And in this worthy endeavour they now find themselves occupying opposite sides of the fence. From this vantage point they see the other as the problem and have little doubt as to where to direct the blame, either explicitly or implicitly.

Underlying the 101 disagreements or conflicting wishes that a couple may have, there are powerful issues at play. In relationships polarization is inevitable. We believe that there are three main areas where individuals are bound to polarize. We shall name them here and then come back to them in more detail later on.

Male and Female

The first area of polarization is perhaps the most obvious one: gender. Cultural, racial, political and social differences affect people, but no difference is so great, so ancient, so archetypal as that of gender. A man and a woman are different. This difference is precisely what creates the magnetic attraction between the two genders and why, like magnets with their different polarities, they are constantly in a dance of searching for each other and then recoiling.

It is certainly tempting to think that it would be easier if the opposite genders did not have to live together and many people today are busy trying out lifestyles that get round this problem. But the biological imperative that the sexual union of male and female creates continues to impel us towards this ongoing difficult experiment.

Besides the obvious physical differences, there are ways in which men and women seem to think, feel and act which confirm the ongoing polarity. In the isolation of a home, these differences can become overwhelming. In the West, couples are unlikely to have the support of a wider and wiser community, one schooled in years of understanding and managing gender differences, as some indigenous cultures have. Often gender differences are unrecognized or, in the wish for political enfranchisement and equality, are thought to be old-fashioned, chauvinistic concepts which a person ought to rise above through right thinking. But it is not so straightforward; it is rarely realized how deep and complex these differences are.

Most important in the gender polarization are the classic differences in approach to sex and feelings and action and emotion. For example, typically the gateway to a woman is her heart. She will want to be emotionally close to her partner before she is ready to relax and open up to sex. Men, on the other hand, mostly find they want sex before they are ready to become vulnerable. They will often interpret a woman's emotionality as the precursor of trouble. Thus emotions and sexuality, which so deeply hold the promise of closeness and union, easily become the battleground of misunderstandings and defensiveness.

Typically – though any generalization is only an inference drawn from patterns observed – men seem to be reactive rather than pro-active in relationships. It can be hard for them to listen to their women talking about whatever is not working for them without going on the defensive or rushing into action and trying to solve the problem. But this rarely seems to be what women want, as Fiona, in Nick Hornby's novel *About a Boy*, protests:

> That's what men think, isn't it, that unless you've got some answer, unless you can say: 'Oh, I know this bloke in Essex Road who can fix that for you,' that it's not worth bothering![2]

We believe that there are intrinsic differences to the genders and that the differences in body affect ways of thinking and relating. We shall expand on this later on. Learning to understand, tolerate and eventually honour our differences is not easy, but it is a great achievement. Nor is it easy to know the extent to which these differences are historical and cultural rather than innate.

When it comes to social and political differences, there are centuries of inequality to be reckoned with. Our religious and social structures have been derived from a base culture where the male's ownership of the female was a principal part of the structure of society. Much of this inequality has only seriously been acknowledged since the advent of feminism. Anger and resentment on the part of women have only begun to be vented. Meanwhile, men logically protest that they are not *personally* responsible.

Even if individuals are not consciously busy with these issues, feelings generated by them will surface in relationship conflict, particularly in terms of how power and vulnerability are employed. The rapid changes in society have meant that the gender roles in Western cultures have been changing too fast for our internal worlds to catch up. There is much confusion; confusion always breeds fear, and fear fans polarization.

Power and Vulnerability

The second issue that causes endless polarization is the dilemma of power and vulnerability. Even though a relationship appears to exist within the arena of love, it is the distribution of power that marks out its dynamics, particularly in this second phase.

The dilemma of power and vulnerability affects both the explicit and implicit power roles in a couple. These include basic issues such as who makes the decisions or who has the last word, as well as more subtle ones, such as who is the one who expresses the problematic side of things or the one who needs to be pleased. It is also about how each partner determines how they will get what they want and how they will deal with not getting it. Dealing with power and vulnerability is complex. It affects almost all communications. For example, gestures which appear innocent yet are full of power may be motivated by resentment, as when hostility is expressed under the cover of apparent humour.

The tension between power and vulnerability reaches into all areas of a couple's life, especially into sex and gender issues, where it crosses over into the area of gender polarization. Here some quite complex subtleties and balancing acts are involved. It is known that in the world of work and politics men have had the dominant role for centuries and that women have suffered under the 'patriarchy'. But as couple counsellors we get to see another side of things too, for instance how incredibly vulnerable many men feel in relation to the opposite gender, or in matters of the home, the heart or sexuality. So it becomes more useful to consider how the power differential affects the system of men and women *together*. Here is a formula to that effect proposed by the writer Sam Keen:

> *In the traditional man-woman game, the payoffs were as follows:*
> *Men got the feeling of power. Women got the power of feeling.*
> *Men got the privilege of public action. Women got the privilege of private being.*
> *Men got responsibility and the guilt that goes with action. Women got innocence and the shame that goes with passivity.*
> *Men got the illusion of control. Women got the illusion of security.*[3]

However, the balancing of power is not simply about gender. If it were, the attempted gender revolution would have got somewhere near to solving it, but it hasn't. The politics of intimacy, though affected by the politics of gender, are structured differently.

The chief difficulty is this: to be intimate with another being specifically requires that you become voluntarily vulnerable. But mostly, men and women alike have grown up learning how to protect themselves and to specifically *avoid* being vulnerable at all costs. To different degrees, we have all been running on psychological automatic pilot, in survival mode. Suffice to say that in terms of dealing with power and vulnerability, mostly it appears that there is a child within us running the show.

It is unlikely that any other life situations will involve us as powerfully as intimate relationships and will make us feel our vulnerability quite so intensely. The polarizations which can occur at the level of power and vulnerability therefore offer a tremendous opportunity: to become conscious of how we have tended to manage these forces in the past and the extent to which our lives are dominated by a fearful child. This can give us the chance to completely rebuild our personalities and the ways in which we engage with the world.

The extent to which the power differentials are distributed in a relationship can be quite alarming. There are many situations in which there appears to be a 'top-dog' and 'under-dog' dynamic, and many subtle ways in which the pecking order changes. Sometimes the one who becomes the 'victim' turns out to have much more power than the one who appears to be in control. Mostly, however, people deal with power by attempting to stay *in control*. Control issues in a relationship boil down to the conflict about who will be the 'parent' (apparently the powerful and important one) and who will be the 'child' (apparently the powerless and needy one). But of course, the partners do not know that this is what they are doing.

This brings us to the third area of polarization.

The Inner Family

Before we met our partner, there was one relationship that was of primary significance to us, although we are usually unaware of its deep effect on us. It is that of our parents. Each and every one of us had our characters fashioned by being involved in the dance between them. It was this relationship, and how we were allotted roles, how we fitted in and managed the tensions between our parents, which in a large part affects all our personalities – our distinct but incomplete signature tunes.

For there is a further dance which causes polarization in our own adult sexual relationships. It is the dilemma between our conscious and unconscious identities. Here we are faced with the difficult dichotomy between the person we like to think we are and the person we have actually become in the process of growing up. This involves all those patterns and tendencies which originate in the past and still haunt us in many disguises. In the self-development culture this is known as 'unfinished business'. It is like a shadowy sack which we drag into all our new relationships until we have a chance to look inside it properly.

Some of these issues we have already touched on. We have hinted that our partners carry aspects of ourselves which we have disowned, denied or not yet developed. But when we polarize, the relationship seems to throw them back in our face with a vengeance. Much of the behaviour which is mirrored back to us concerns how we dealt with being a vulnerable child in our family of origin and how our parents dealt with us, or with those aspects of our childishness which were not wanted in the family. And so in our current relationships we look for another chance to get the support that we did not get the first time around. But in order for us to discover just what kind of support we need, our partner must first let us down.

Being modern people and claiming the privileges of adulthood earlier and earlier, we may imagine that we have already outgrown such childish deficiencies. But that is wishful thinking. They are deeply ingrained in us. We may think it a worn-out cliché that we are bound to marry our mothers or fathers, but on reflection the notion has more going for it than we would like to admit.

As children we learned our first lessons in love from our parents. We had no choice, for we were brought into the world through their sexual relationship and were raised within its emotional atmosphere. This was our learning ground and we learned our lessons well. So when we grow up and are faced with the prospect of starting our own family we automatically tend to act like our parents, even if we have invested a lifetime in trying to be different.

Without knowing it, we also seek out many of the same characteristics in our partners which we have been trying to reconcile in our original loved ones. We fall into these traps as though a part of us seems to sense quite precisely what we may need from our partners. The paradox is that we *have* to fall into the trap we set ourselves. Otherwise we might miss the opportunity to eventually resolve our unfinished business. In other words, we would continue to apply the behaviour and thought patterns we learned as a child and these will inevitably have shortcomings when applied to adult intimate relationships.

But this is being wise after the event: the problem is that when we begin to feel that we have got ourselves right back into old situations we thought we had outgrown, we panic and polarize.

For now we need to further consider the complex ways in which we try to manage all the difficult dynamics of dancing in the dark with the partner who is no longer the one we thought we had chosen.

He glances up and notices that she looks stressed. So he asks her if there's something on her mind. At first she says, 'No,' but when he tries the third time, she says she wants to talk.

So she talks, and he tries to listen.

But he can't. He feels blamed. What she wants to talk about is him – how he seems not to care about her, or the relationship, and how everything in his life seems to have more priority than her, and she is sick of it.

He feels accused and wants to defend himself. 'But you know, when we're apart I long for you.'

'And when we're together you ignore me,' she counters.

He tries to reason and to come up with something else in his defence. But she will have none of it. He gets angry.

This does not help things at all.

The weekend passes grimly.

Finally, when they are both exhausted, he says, 'I love you.'
She looks at him and weeps.
He reaches out with his hand, leaning forward.
She withdraws and angrily answers: 'It's too late.'
When he expresses his commitment, she backs away. Now he has woken up to how serious it is, but his intensity is too much for her. He declares: 'Come on, I simply refuse to play this game of backing off.'
But he already has backed off, and he knows it, and for now it's too late.
They both feel alone, in a prison of their own making.

Together or Apart?

In our practice we see all aspects of coupledom, but some things are universal. When people first come to see us, they are convinced that their relationship is no longer working for them. And they invariably feel bad about this.

More often than not, the individuals imagine that it might work if only their partner were different. Although they have tried to make their partner see sense and change, it has failed. For most couples, the impetus to come to counselling is a sense of helplessness. They feel hopeless; they feel let down. The presenting symptoms are usually a variation on a theme: it may be that the conflict is too much or one partner has had an affair or is threatening to leave. Sometimes a deadening dullness has set in, suffocating both, sometimes for different reasons. Failure and disappointment are the overwhelming conclusions. Despair or resignation are on the way in.

But have they failed? Sure, they have failed to manage their relationship in the way that they thought it *ought* to be. We prefer to say that their 'maintenance level' has collapsed, which is why they are seeking help. Usually they want us to do some restoration and repair work. But intimate relationships are powerful and mysterious. They pull people into a vortex, which is usually a lot more than they bargained for.

As counsellors, we regularly hear how at least one of the partners wants the relationship to be like it was in the beginning and that they are puzzled as to how they got to this stage of failure. The fear and disappointment make people want either to return to the way that it was, or cut and run. And since return is never possible, only the latter seems realistic.

According to recent British statistics, most couples who seek divorce, mediation or couple counselling have been in a committed relationship for about three to seven years. This is fairly early on in the life of a potential long-term relationship and many social commentators wonder why this is so. We believe that this is exactly the right time for some of the psychological disappointments to have kicked in and that relationships are then poised to move to a new and more creative level. Since couples are neither expecting things to collapse, let alone an opportunity to follow, it is invariably a time of great bewilderment. Nevertheless, there are also some very practical reasons for there being problems at this time, which are worth briefly exploring.

Many couples who enter what they intend to be a life-long relationship are likely to have started a family within the first seven years. The fundamental change that this brings to a couple cannot ever be overstated. It seems to be one of those things in life that no amount of knowledge can ever truly prepare a person for. However wanted a child is, its arrival completely changes the lives of its parents. A newborn child is awesome and mysterious by virtue of the sheer presence of its being. But the utter dependence and power of the human infant puts unimaginable strain on the parents' time and energy – especially when they are in the lonely situation of the nuclear family.

When both parents are exhausted and occupied with their children it is extremely difficult for them to realize that their relationship needs care and attention too. When stress hits, their relationship will easily become the last priority. And how *do* they take time out for themselves? On top of this, when they experience each other as a real live mum and dad to a real live child, some of the attraction they once felt seems to get lost. Parenthood can kill sexual passion stone dead. Family life and relationship can therefore easily crystallize as two mutually incompatible projects.

Even without a family, the tendency to develop problems after a few years of settling down together is noticeable in most of the couples that we see in therapy. But we are increasingly also seeing couples who run into trouble much earlier on – well inside the three to seven year cycle. These tend to be people with experience of previous relationship break-ups who are perhaps on their second or third attempt at trying to fulfil a long-term commitment. We imagine that in such couples the psychological challenges strike earlier and harder. It is almost as if they have fast-forwarded their patterns and have moved rapidly from attraction to repulsion. Since we believe that partners have serious business with each other, each trying to recover something vitally important, we consider it a shame if they do not have the opportunity to complete it – especially those couples who are beginning to experience meeting the same problems repeatedly with different partners. Otherwise they may remain actors in the tragedy of the 'serial monogamist'.

At the other end of the spectrum, those couples who have been together for much longer and have raised a family can run into trouble when their children fly the nest. Now left to their own devices, the parents begin to feel at a loss. During the years spent on child-rearing they lost sight of one another as an individual man and woman: they became 'mum and dad'. Now that they are no longer able to relate to each other through the children, they become familiar strangers, occupying the same spaces but not the same worlds. The departing children leave a gap in which the parents are haunted by a strange sense of having grown apart. Sometimes they do not mention it; sometimes they will part so as not to feel their emptiness.

It seems to us that intimate relationships provide chances to learn particular lessons and that your life *wants* you to learn them. Whatever these lessons may be, they are for individuals to discover themselves. It can be helpful when their partners or their therapists reflect back aspects of themselves with which they are not yet reconciled. But this is not the end of the story. It is relatively easy to see what other people can't see, but much harder to recognize your own blind spots, and it is never easy to learn when under stress.

How should a couple who are in deep crisis persuade themselves that they are on the edge of a great adventure? At such a time it is very hard for them to see that their relationship may be nudging them deeper into themselves, further into the dangerous waters of intimacy, in order to be transformed. Moreover, not all couples will have the desire, determination or courage to make such a journey. Sometimes one partner may consistently refuse to work on the relationship and a parting of ways may seem best, at other times there are definite reasons to believe that a relationship should end – especially in relationships which have explicit and recurrent violent or abusive elements built into them. In such cases, getting out can be a life saver. But in general the dawning of relationship crisis seems to us to signal that a new phase is beginning and though the partners may be strongly tempted to toss the disappointing catch back into the water, there are several reasons why this could turn out to be a mistake.

Let us be perfectly clear here. We are *not* saying that everyone should stay together whatever happens. Each relationship is unique and what works for one may not work for another. Sometimes people must act on the realization that they have made a mistake, whether they learn from it or not. Sometimes the price of both partners having to change in order to shift the relationship to another level may be too high. Sometimes, if a person really begins to change, the choices which they made earlier cannot necessarily be sustained. And if one person is developing at a different rate from the other it can also be tempting to want to move on – but this one is particularly tricky, especially if applied without a serious attempt to explore what is happening.

What we are saying is this: there are very good reasons to think more than twice before parting. According to Jan Laithwaite of Relate, 50 per cent of couples who split up a long-term relationship later regret their decision.[4] When considering separation couples usually benefit if they are able to recruit a professional to help them think some of the issues through. It is far cheaper than divorce. Our reasons for trying to work on a relationship are not moral, but psychological, or 'psycho-ecological'. In other words, it is a lot better to invest in your relationship than in your lawyer, and whatever work you put in is likely to be recycled and feed the whole! There are also powerful pragmatic reasons for not parting as soon as it begins to feel hopeless.

Not in Front of the Children

Most importantly, if there are children involved they will want their parents to stay together. Those of us who split up families made countless mistakes. Many of them were committed with the best intentions, under the pressure of forces which made things near impossible to get right, but however a break-up is managed, it will rent lives.

It is often thought that it is bad for children to witness conflict between parents. We increasingly think that this is mistaken. What *is* bad is for children to conclude that their parents cannot manage conflict. Using children as go-betweens or shields is clearly harmful. But having parents who demonstrate that they are able to undergo relationship difficulties *and* come out the other side is a huge advantage. It will become hardwired into the child's mind as a tool for managing problems in their own life. Imagine that in your own family your father and mother had shown by their example that conflicts happen in relationship – it's normal – and that people can get through them safely, without denial or domination. You may well have seen that this process made them grow and that their relationship became stronger and deeper. What difference would that have made to your life?

Staying together 'for the children' is not necessarily a creative solution. Working on a relationship *for the sake of all involved* is a different story. Showing that relationship skills are important and not to be taken for granted is a hard but useful lesson. Parents who cannot resolve their conflicts may end up teaching their children that relationships can't last, that it's all too difficult. This can exacerbate the tendency towards the short attention-span style of living which our consumerist world seems to want to make the norm. In a healthy future, the emphasis would be on demonstrating the value of managing conflict rather than returning to the old model of keeping things under wraps. Facing problems helps, but repression or guilt never do.

Whenever parents separate and recombine into new families, it involves the children in worlds of complexity where the tensions are often irresolvable. We have already stated our belief that step-families are some of the hardest combinations imaginable. Those who have not yet been part of one may find it hard to imagine just how difficult they are. In such new combinations children are driven to get their needs met by even more manipulation than they would otherwise employ in the normal difficulties of family life. Here is Tony Parsons again:

The worst thing about splitting up ... [is that] it makes children hide their hearts. It teaches them how to move between separate worlds. It turns them into little diplomats.[5]

So, if splitting is not the first or only option, what does a couple do?

CHAPTER 6

The Chase

In our search for love we find we have to let go of the very thing we are clinging to – the idea of love itself.

James Hillman

If partners are not to split up when the forces of repulsion hurl the partners to opposite ends of the room, they will have to manage the difficulties of this energy the best they can. The instinctual reaction, when the good feelings of the honeymoon period have ceased, is to retreat to what we call 'a safe distance for intimacy'.

At the start of a relationship we exhibit a kind of vulnerability which we normally daren't show. The safety produced by being in love has a strong effect on the child who emotionally still lives inside us. 'Now my needs will be met, now I'll finally be loved for who I am,' this child secretly hopes and we relax. In this relaxation, we permit other parts of ourselves to shine through. Next, we stop being quite so attentive to our partner, so keenly interested in their thoughts and feelings. Over time we easily fall into the habit of taking the other for granted. Both notice it, both dislike it. As the polarization begins, the newfound sense of safety is disturbed.

Having dared to open up for the sake of love, we now recoil. When the safety is lost, a lonely unwanted part inside us concludes that we were not good enough after all, not truly lovable. No longer feeling safe to live with an open heart, we gradually close it again. Sometimes we slam it too. The fear of conflict, or of an intimacy never before known, makes us return to familiar patterns of behaviour which helped us to feel safe in the past.

By 'familiar', we do not mean that we choose these patterns consciously. Rather, we retreat to a psychological default mechanism that was most likely constructed in our family of origin. Such patterns have at their core a strategy to manipulate the other in order to avoid becoming vulnerable or dependent. They have many forms. If a scriptwriter were commissioned to draft a movie about this side of relationships, they might come up with lines like the following:

'I deserve to get what I want without having to ask for it.'
'I'll give him what he wants but nothing of myself.'
'I'll not be the needy one now that I have got her (to play that role).'
'I'll act stupid so he won't be threatened and will let me have my way.'
'I won't care about you, then you can't hurt me.'
'It's no use expecting anything from you, so I won't!'
'See if I care!'
'I'll be whatever you want, just don't leave me.'

There are endless varieties of these stances taken to create a 'safe distance' in an intimate relationship.

It's important to note that this manipulative behaviour is not driven by malice, but by fear. Fear is a powerful and useful emotion which signals danger. Such an emotional alarm system helped our ancestors stay alive when they lived amongst wild animals. These days, the wildest creature we are likely to come across in our everyday dealings is our partner! And of course, in relationships there will be fear: of losing love, and paradoxically, sometimes fear of having it. The bottom line is that the nearness of love evokes fear. But fear doesn't help much in matters of the heart.

We have already established that being intimate involves being vulnerable. The invitation to be vulnerable brings with it the fear of dependence. And this fear is very difficult to deal with, because although we all longed to be cared for and to be freely dependent when we were children, we probably did not have all those needs fully met. We will then have made a subconscious decision to avoid becoming too dependent in the future. But when we enter an intimate relationship our original hopes and longings become reawakened – only, it seems, to be once more disappointed. This is what sets off the danger signals.

Partners who learned to deny their feelings of vulnerability and their willingness to be dependent may be shocked at the uncanny precision with which they resurface in their partner. This can, however, be turned to good use. Having had to disown their vulnerability, or their hopelessness, or their depression, they can manage to construct a role for themselves by becoming saddled with someone who is clearly more of an emotional and problematic person than they are. Now they can safely appear to the world as the logical, competent, caring or non-addicted one. At the same time, they give their partner the devoted parental caring that they actually crave for themselves. This is known in counselling as 'co-dependency'. It is a powerful and addictive form of compensation. It's like a child trying to give love to a parent so that the parent can learn to love them back. It seldom works, but co-dependent lovers can keep going forever in this 'safe distance' for intimacy.

Eventually, however, this pattern will take its toll. Those who become carers in this fashion will become resentful and depleted. Placating, satisfying or criticizing the never-ending neediness and demands of their partner will provide a role, but leave them feeling empty. On top of this, they often have problems with acknowledging feelings and asking for what they want. They are unaware of their own unmet dependency needs and the longing of their inner child to be loved and cared for. Co-dependents, although focused on caring for the partner, are invariably driven by the motivation to have something for themselves, without properly acknowledging their own needs.

A Note on Needs

The need to belong and to be loved is innate to the human psyche. We cannot get round it. Being mothered in childhood was our first opportunity for this. Once we know that we belong and are loved well enough, we are satisfied, we are secure. Then, sooner or later, the security becomes stifling and we are ready to have our next psychological need satisfied: that of autonomy, or independence. Autonomy is the ability to function more or less on our own, to make our own choices, to do and to want. It is about freedom and self-determination. Human beings are never fully independent – no man is an island, as they say – but the need to be autonomous has to be fairly well satisfied as a precursor for adult psychological health. Thus we build self-esteem and self-worth, which are the basis for being able to truly love another person.

Life is rarely ideal, however, and most of us will have had to make compromises – or sometimes sacrifices – to satisfy our needs both to belong and to be autonomous. For example, if as children we were over-controlled or made special by one or both parents, we grow up learning to be a 'good boy' or 'good girl' according to prevailing conditions and expectations. So we fulfil these conditions in order to get love and a sense of belonging. In such a case, belonging is achieved at the expense of autonomy – a compromise which necessitates a degree of self-betrayal.

In a different scenario, children who are neglected, physically or emotionally, or who have immature parents, or who lose their home too early, will develop an independent and self-reliant demeanour. But such children will have achieved their autonomy at the expense of their need to belong. It is a similar but complementary compromise and self-betrayal to the one described above.

These are but some of the ways in which we cope with the difficulty of balancing our innate need to belong with our need for freedom.[1]

Intimate relationships bring into drastic focus how we solved this dilemma in the past. Since our relationships can confront us with the deals we habitually make and can force us to re-examine our attitudes to our needs, we have a chance to review our default behaviour. In the meantime, as long as the inner child's need for safety continues to be in charge of the adult's availability for intimate relationship, the safe distance for intimacy is rarely deeply satisfying.

Things may yet have to get worse before they get better.

She knew from the way she was dialling his work number that she was anxious. She was pressing the number keys just a little bit too hard. His response to her over-cheery 'Hello, darling' confirmed her suspicions. She could detect a distance in his voice, as if speaking to her were the most tremendous interruption to his busy important life. Damn.

'I'm sorry,' she tried, 'are you busy? Am I disturbing you?'

'No, not at all,' he said. But he was curt and she was sure he was lying. 'Was there something particular you wanted?'

'I just thought I'd check in with you,' she said calmly by means of her I-can-handle-anything-it's-not-that-I'm-needy voice.

'Great,' he replied and there was a moment of silence.

'As a matter of fact, I've just seen a really lovely flat, just off Shepherds Hill,' she continued, trying not to be too enthusiastic. 'It would be just perfect for us, it even has a room you could use as a study, and maybe later on...'

'Look,' he interrupted, 'to be honest, I really do have quite a bit on right now and I thought we'd said we'd wait till after Christmas before we'd even think about looking for somewhere new.'

And inside she just died a little, and felt stranded, like an empty bottle washed up on a drab windy beach somewhere. So she just hung up on him and reached for a cigarette.

More Wild Creatures: The Dance of the Pushme-Pullyou

One way couples attempt to manage their anxiety and balance their individual hierarchy of needs is by dancing an odd dance. This dance has paradoxical and often perverse steps. It involves one person pushing for something while the other refuses to give it. It may be love, or attention, or understanding, more power, more sex – anything. It does not matter what it is – it can be something sensible or something quite irrational. It's the unobtainability that is important. The one who does not get it starts to chase the one who won't give it. Both parties become increasingly frustrated and convinced of how unfairly they are being treated. This makes them either chase or keep out of reach even more. There is no end to this dance and although we say it is a way of 'managing', it is not ultimately satisfying and it feels very painful and hopeless.

The most obvious conclusion for both partners involved in this dance is that the other is the problem. These days, couples may even go along to a therapist to get professional support for living with this impossible creature that they have had the misfortune to be stabled with. Luckily, most counsellors won't buy into this version, as they will want to look at the relationship as a system. They will want to look at the meaning of all the steps in this dance. Most likely they will recognize it as something psychologists call 'the distancer-pursuer dynamic'.

The syndrome was first noted by systemic therapists in Palo Alto, California, in the mid-1960s. At that time the focus was on partners who nagged and partners who withdrew – classically a husband withdrawing from a nagging wife. Couples were seen as regulating the distance between them by polarizing – one wanting space or separateness and the other wanting closeness or relational activity. But the more one chases, the more the other runs.[2] There is no solution.

To understand this dance we have to think of the three elements involved in this system: the relationship and the two individuals. With the onset of polarization the relationship enters its first major phase of challenge for the individuals involved. Each partner is tested to see whether they really want a relationship and what they will give up in order to achieve it. As the relationship starts to close in on them they have to consider some difficult questions. How much closeness do they want? How much do they want to be a unit? How will they cope with their conflicting needs for belonging and independence? Deep in their psyches their prime fears are being aroused by these questions. For some – usually the men – it will be the fear of being swamped, engulfed, losing their individuality, their independence. For others – classically the women – it will be the fear of being abandoned, marginalized, ignored or deserted.

The central dilemma is: *How do individuals live both separate and joint lives within a relationship?*

In her book *Intimate Partners*, Maggie Scarf describes the difficulty:

Generally speaking, when couples are experiencing a great deal of distress, confusion and unhappiness, the underlying conflict is about trying to remain in an intimate relationship while being a full, whole, separate human being simultaneously. The wish to pursue one's own interests and goals and the wish to pursue interests and goals that are shared with the mate feel as if they are totally incompatible. One feels that one can either be fully autonomous or be intimate with the partner, but being both at once is impossible.[3]

Another way of putting this is to say that there is competition between the needs of the relationship and those of the individuals. The partners attempt to manage this difficulty by the distancer-pursuer dance. The distancer sacrifices belonging needs and fears engulfment; the pursuer sacrifices autonomy needs and fears abandonment.

The invariability of the rules – the pursuer chases the distancer but never catches up – shows that both players are in collusion, already playing a joint rather than an individual game. It is as if the fisherman, recoiling from the monster he has caught, starts to run away and thinks that he is being chased. But in reality he is still holding onto his fishing line and both the catcher and the caught are in it together. We can establish life-long patterns of one wanting more and the other less, one wanting closeness and the other space. We can play these games till we die, and many couples do.

In the children's story *Doctor Dolittle*, Hugh Lofting invented a strange beast called the Pushme-Pullyou. It looked like a llama, but had a head at each end. It would begin to go in one direction, but then the other end would move and it would start off in the opposite direction. There would be a lot of activity, but it would get nowhere. This is how we see the distancer-pursuer dance.

The Pushme-Pullyou helps us remember that when the energy seems to be focused in a chase in one direction, there will most likely be another context where it goes off in the other. Couples where one party is seriously engaged in the pursuit of emotional intimacy, for example, may reverse roles where sex is concerned. Traditionally, women were seen as the ones most interested in emotional closeness. In sexual matters, on the other hand, men tended to be the pursuers and women the distancers – unless the man was using the strategy of controlling the woman's need for time together by denying her sex. Once upon a time, women kept a close watch on how much sex they permitted, as it was one of the few areas in which they had power. Here their sexual distancing is recognizable as a counter-step that belongs to their dance of emotional pursuit. It is an age-old ritual and one apparently practised by primates. Dudley Young, the author of a book on apes and the origin of religion and war, tells us:

> The male chimpanzee chases the female until she catches him.[4]

The body of the Pushme-Pullyou reminds us of a further rule in the dance. Any movement or change at one end produces a movement or change at the other, and then the whole creature realigns itself. This is the law of systems and the Pushme-Pullyou is a powerful system. For example, let us imagine that there is a dance around having sex. If the partner who is pushing for more sex is reliably frustrated by the other's 'no', then things may change dramatically when that partner takes a new position. If the pursuer suddenly receives a consistent 'yes', then some of the excitement of the chase may dramatically disappear and the pursuer may turn out not to be so keen after all.

Likewise, within an argument many shifting movements are corrected by subsequent responses. One partner will push the other away until they begin to feel that they have lost control or gone too far. Then they will become the pursuer, fervently attempting to apologize to the now unreachable partner. More subtly, you can see the dynamic at work in the way that one partner tentatively reaches out to the other, but withdraws the moment they anticipate a rejection.

Even though from the outside this dance seems to be a restless affair, from the perspective of the system itself there is an in-built tendency for things to remain the same, to reproduce a reliable, if comfortless stability. If one partner appears to be depressed it is likely that the other will be overactive. In the areas where one partner is over-functioning, the other is likely to be under-functioning. Thus the Pushme-Pullyou balances things out – if one head is up, then the other must be down. Such precise corrections to imbalances usually relate to the couple's initial attraction for each other. Between them they have all the qualities to make up one healthy functioning individual, but shared between them it makes an endless battle.

For the dance to stop, both parties have to *want* to get to the bottom of things. And this is where the real paradoxical and perverse steps come in. Couples have a surprising capacity for creating and also tolerating frustration and misery. It may be that they really don't want the relationship to change. The one who endlessly complains about the other, for example, may be staking their claim to not being the one who should change. There may be a huge payoff for being the one whose life is crippled by being shackled to an impossible mate. Or again, the one who never gets what they want may need to keep the pattern going, because if they got what they apparently long for, they would not know what to do.

Writer Sheldon Kopp says that there are some people who 'prefer the security of known misery to the misery of unfamiliar insecurity'.[5] This suggests that people can sometimes have a perverse psychological investment in having relationship difficulties. It's not that people are enjoying themselves by playing frustrating games with their spouses, but these games can answer their need for security. Really changing any part of this dance will involve changing everything. It will involve a loss of security, plus the determination to get right to the heart of the matter. The implications of putting up with a partner's behaviour can be far less threatening than having to recognize and change one's own behaviour. The dance remains potent precisely because nothing will change unless both partners are able to see the effect of the steps they habitually make and are willing to risk doing it differently. A *real* change in one of the partners would seriously threaten the sense of belonging which both are busy serving. To break free, both have to understand why they cling to such crude solutions to the problem of dependence and independence.

You Can Lean on Me, Baby

Behind every step in the dance of the Pushme-Pullyou is the central dilemma of being dependent or independent. This is a complex issue. How we respond to it chiefly depends on what messages we received in our families of origin at a time when we had no option but to be dependent children. Pursuers who push for relationship and belonging needs may have concluded early on that showing their neediness was a means of preventing abandonment by the all-important other. But as adults, the same behaviour is likely to result in their being avoided. Distancers, on the other hand, under the banner of freedom, carry the belief that showing vulnerability and needs will get you nowhere, apart from being left alone or abandoned. They experience their partner's neediness as a threat to their hard-won, if compromised, independence.

Ideally, in an intimate relationship, both types would want to grow out of this dilemma and establish a healthy interdependency. But this involves much psychological maturity. The prerequisite is a certain degree of being at ease with oneself. Maggie Scarf suggests that behind the distancer-pursuer cycle both partners have a problem with being alone. If they were alone they would have to deal with all the things that they are now attributing to their partner. For example, on examination, the pursuers' versions of intimacy regularly turn out to be their own wish to be listened to, understood and met. In this way personal goals are assumed to be those of the relationship – and the partner is then accused of failing to provide them.

> Although she desires closeness more than anything else in the world, the pursuer wants it in her own fashion, in her own time, and in her own way. She needs to have him be there for her, but has trouble hearing things that reminds her of his separateness and independence. They both, it might be said, have a similar problem, which we can all find so difficult, of dealing with human aloneness.[6]

Although Scarf cites the classic version, with the woman cast in the pursuer role, there are signs that this has been changing in recent generations. A recent study focuses on a dramatic reversal of this pattern in couples presenting for therapy.[7] The increased economic opportunities for women, coupled with their tendency to identify with their fathers' apparently greater degree of independence in preference to their mothers' domesticity, have produced a new wave of female distancers. They are often conveniently paired with rather needy, less ambitious or placative males. Nevertheless, women are still represented as those who are most likely to be dissatisfied with their relationships and they are more likely than men to want to separate.

But whoever is doing the chasing or the running, it's still the same old dance and nothing really changes by just reversing the roles. Even in the traditional casting the man was expected to be the pursuer to begin with, albeit under the guise of hunting for sex. But once the wedding bells had tolled, he would be on the emotional runway.

Distancers have their own reasons for reacting in the way they do. The demands of an intimate relationship will clash with their desire to be self-sufficient and left in peace. They frequently turn out to be extremely threatened by the closeness of intimacy and terrified of acknowledging their own needs. On the run from their needs, they feel exasperated by the neediness of their partner, since they are desperate not to come in contact with their own. However at ease such a person might appear to be with aloneness, one should not be fooled: such aloneness often relates to being pursued. There is a safety in being pursued by someone who *never* leaves you alone.

The ability to be genuinely alone is the mark of the ability to also be with another person, to be interdependent. Both achievements are badges of maturity and we all have to make our mistakes first. A person who can be *interdependent* is one who is no longer compromising for the sake of belonging, has a degree of self-knowledge and is able to honour the uniqueness of the other.

Settling for What You Can Get

In couple dynamics we notice two primary ways of solving an impasse in the dependence/independence dilemma. On the one hand, I can force the partner to become dependent so that '*I* am not the dependent one.' Alternatively, I can refuse to take responsibility and grow up psychologically, so that 'I get my share of comfortable dependency which I could not have in my childhood.' Such 'solutions' can become long-lasting bases for relationship and constitute what we call 'static bonding patterns'.

We will discuss bonding patterns in detail in the next chapter. Meanwhile, couple counsellor Tony Gough has spotted several such static solutions, which he calls 'unhealthy models of marriage',[8] and has given them interesting names. Here are three of them.

First, there is the 'Siamese Twins' marriage, similar to what we call a 'Babes in the Wood' relationship. This is a relationship based on not differentiating and never disagreeing, so that the mutual unnamed co-dependence prevents either party from feeling dependent. Gough likens this kind of an arrangement to Howard and Hilda, the couple portrayed in the late eighties TV comedy programme *Ever Decreasing Circles*:

> Howard and Hilda will never need counselling – until, that is, one of them decides to become a real, separate individual. At this point, their marriage will face a real crisis.

Next he describes the 'Doll's House' marriage, from Ibsen's play – a powerful description of a typical Victorian marriage. In this, the husband has all the power on the outside and keeps his wife as a sort of slave; he sees her as weak and helpless, while she retains all the power on the inside. Echoing Sam Keen's assessment of the payoffs in the traditional power game, Gough reveals:

> 'Doll's house' marriages are based on a kind of confidence trick. The wife uses her power in order to support her husband's need to be in control of the relationship. She protects her husband from the unpalatable truth that he needs looking after.

Gough eerily suggests that in these cases one of the only ways in which the husband can receive support is to get ill, because a big strong man who's ill can still 'entertain the illusion that it's his illness that being looked after, not him'.

Finally, he describes the 'Peter Pan and Wendy' marriage, which is the converse of the previous type. We see many examples of this style in our consulting rooms. Here the wife assumes the dominating role because the husband is either afraid of his power or wants to stay a little boy, or both. Maybe he is too fearful, too vain or trying hard to be a 'new man'. In the traditional version he would be the 'hen-pecked' Andy Capp or Basil Fawlty, always trying to avoid his wife's displeasure, but endless recreating it. Freedom is getting out to the pub; safety is having her waiting with a rolling pin. In this way he never has to assume responsibility. She remains mummy and he doesn't have to grow up. Game, set and match. In the more modern version he tries endlessly to placate her, but nothing works. It can last indefinitely. Here is Gough's analysis:

> While each partner keeps to the rules, all will be well. But when one changes, or matures, or simply gets to the end of their tether (and its usually 'Wendy/Wife' who reaches this first), the fat is in the fire.

Peter Pan will need to grow up, but Wendy will have to let him, and this involves the serious loss of a well-defined role.

In the next chapter we will look more closely into how our ideals and fantasies of mummies and daddies and children inside us can get all mixed up, particularly when the conflict begins to heat up.

CHAPTER 7

Patterns of the Past

People think that relationships are about happiness. But they're not. They're about transformation.

Joseph Campbell

The screen on the television fluttered and then went blank. He got up from the sofa, switched off all the lamps and climbed the stairs.

'Great,' he thought, seeing the light escaping from the half-closed bedroom door, 'she's still awake.' He slipped out of his clothes and slid in beside his wife, who smiled at him, looking up from her book, and then went on reading. She smelled good. Her regular breathing and the outline of her body beneath the sheets had a strong effect on him. He reached out a hand and caressed her smooth belly. She smiled again, so he moved closer and began gently to nibble her ear.

'Not just now, OK? I want to read,' she said, moving her head away.

He said nothing. His heart was pounding and his body began to freeze. She remained immersed in her book, as if he weren't there.

Finally, he broke the silence. 'I might as well sleep in the other room,' he said.

She put down the book and gave him her long severe look.

'What is the problem?' she said with studied impatience (as if she didn't know).

'I just felt close to you and wanted to make love with you, but I see I'm in the way,' he said in his best innocent voice.

'And if I am not in the mood just now?' she demanded. 'Or is it all just about you again?'

'But you never want to, there's always some reason or other. I think you've got a real problem with sexuality. No wonder your last marriage didn't work out.'

'Don't you talk to me about sexual hang-ups,' she answered back. 'All you want is a mother to take care of your every little whim. Well, this lady ain't your mother, get it? Even if the last one was.' Now she was sitting up straight, while he hung his head in a long-suffering way.

'OK, I've got the message,' he said, rising to his feet with a burst of energy. 'Just remember all I wanted was some loving time with you, not another bloody lecture from the Ice Queen,' he added, before he stormed out, slamming the door and stomping down the corridor to take final refuge in the cold guest bedroom.

Another night of domestic war.

The Inner Family in Action

How often do such scenes repeat themselves in houses up and down the land? What started as a dream of love ends as a battle-field. Both parties feel aggrieved, lonely and sexually frustrated. If either regrets the things that they said, they keep it to themselves – at least for the time being. In the morning they may apologize and try again. But sometimes one partner will take days to come round and in the meantime they are building up a stock of bad memories. Those are very hard to eradicate.

What was really going on in this exchange? Let's take a closer look.

In this apparently simple clash of wills between the man's attempt to make love and his wife's wish to stay reading, many different levels of the couple's personality are fired into action. The trigger point for him is her refusing his advances. Even though she does it in a perfectly reasonable way, he has a strong reaction, both physically and emotionally. The chief problem is that he begins to feel rejected. All of us struggle to handle feelings of rejection when they come to us. Men in particular can take it hard when their offers of love-making are spurned and can become very vulnerable and hurt.

As soon as the feelings of rejection and vulnerability come over him, our male responds in a sulky way. In this mode it is as if he has turned into a little boy who cannot get his way. Now any woman will agree that possibly the least sexy thing to have in her bed is a sulky little boy. It is definitely not a 'turn on' for her. A woman does not want sex with a child. She wants it with an adult man who desires her and who is not going to be upset by the slightest response she makes. So his childish reaction *guarantees* that they will not have sex. It is a set-up for loss.

Not only does the man react like a spoiled child, but there is also another tone to his voice – it is haughty, as if he were looking down on her, as if *she* were the child and he some superior grown-up who knows better. And to this she does respond. She reacts to him with barely disguised irritation: she has been through this movie before and is now in her irritated but long-suffering mode. So he shifts gear and tries to be a sweeter and more innocent child, since that has been known to win her round before. But she will have nothing of it. It just gets her goat even more – as he probably intends. His sweetness masks a certain manipulativeness, designed to portray her as a with-holding mother figure, which is how the child in him now experiences her. And on it goes – at every stage of the game they both up the ante a little more, increasing the hostility in each exchange until it is totally out of control.

What is remarkable in this conflict is that both partners adopt styles which have the character of either children or parent figures. Why should this be?

The answer lies in the very earliest moments of human consciousness. Unlike other vertebrates, humans are born extremely helpless and dependent on others. Where foals are on their feet and curious within minutes, human babies need a good nine months before they take their first steps and several years before they can fend for themselves in any but the most rudimentary way. We are extremely vulnerable and dependent on our fellows, especially our parents, for a considerable period of time. Perhaps this vulnerability is nature's price for our large self-reflective neo-cortex, upright position and unmatched manual dexterity, for these features give us the unbeatable evolutionary advantage. But vulnerability and dependence remain difficult issues for us as we grow up.

At the same time, it seems that nature has designed us to expect unconditional love and protection from our parental caretakers. It is as if we are programmed to be interdependent social beings who expect a welcome and good treatment from those who are already in the world.[1] During the period when our bodies and minds are doing the most developing, we rely on the powerful adults around us for everything – not just food, physical shelter and stimulus, but above all for love and approval. The psychological effect of this dependence is that in order to encourage our protectors and to cope with their inevitable shortcomings, we learn to apply a certain amount of manipulation, through facial expressions, tone of voice, and so on.

At the same time an internal process of identification and character building is taking place. The logic works like this: whatever is strong and coping becomes linked with the powerful parents we see outside us, and whatever is weak and dependent becomes associated with the child we are. As time goes on, those parts of our own psyche which are powerful acquire *parental* status and those which are vulnerable acquire *child* status.

A parent has the function of keeping a child safe and of helping it to regulate its energies until it is able to take over those functions for itself. The internalized parent has similar functions within the psyche, those of *protection* and *control*. In this way, the child has a functional parent part built into its imagination for support while it develops its own autonomous self. But it also has a complementary child part, which stands for all the qualities that need protection, such as vulnerability and dependence. And this is where the trouble lies.

Our nineteenth-century forefathers did not greatly approve of the qualities of childhood, such as unbridled emotionality, innocence, spontaneity and messiness. In consequence, being a child in Western society has not been a particularly attractive option until very recently.[2] As we saw earlier, our psyches take a long time to catch up with the changes in society. And so there remains a consensus pressure that encourages individuals to identify with the parent parts of their psyche and to disown the child parts.

This creates a severe internal tension which is usually resolved by the tendency not to appear vulnerable or dependent and to be self-reliant or aloof or even domineering. It amounts to a parody of adulthood, further distorted because these qualities of parenthood are conceived from a child's perspective. The inner parent turns out to be mostly a fantasy adult – what a parent is 'supposed' to be – modelled on the child's experience of its own caretakers. They, in turn, were most likely struggling to be adults themselves, from the perspective of their own suppressed inner children.

Inner parent figures have yet a further function. Because our biological goal is to become adults, as boys and girls grow out of infancy they need to identify with their fathers and mothers.

To greater or lesser degrees, they inevitably succeed in this — even when a person does their utmost not to turn out like their father or mother. Even when people go to all possible lengths of rebellion and contradictory lifestyles, they will unfailingly develop *some* of their parents' characteristics, especially in terms of unconscious behaviour patterns. It is a reality (and often feels like a tragedy!) which we all have to face. Leaving aside the genetic inheritance, the likeness is of course due to our exposure to our parents' attitudes, beliefs and behaviour during our childhood.

The emphasis is therefore firmly in favour of suppressing the inner child in favour of the inner parent. This area of internal conflict is well documented in the psychological literature. It has inspired several theories, from the complex internal dynamics of the psychoanalytical school of Object Relations[3] to the simple but useful models of Transactional Analysis.[4] The latter proposes that we can usefully speak of an adult psyche as composed of three primary poles — adult, parent and child.

The adult part is that which grown-up people intend to present to the world. On the inside, however, there is a child part, compiled of disowned, vulnerable, foolish and messy aspects of the person. Alongside this is the parent part, whose function is to keep the inner child in check, thereby keeping the person safe from hurt, dependence and regression in daily life. In practice, there is usually an internal conflict between the parent part and the child part. Although he used different terms, this approximates to Freud's starting-point, when he described humans as struggling with the unconscious tension between civilization and instinct, mediated by the Superego.

While this inner set-up seems to be almost universal in our society and comprises the bread-and-butter work of psychotherapists, it is still not common knowledge outside psychological circles. It is extremely unecological in terms of its effect, since keeping the inner balance stable consumes a lot of psychological energy. In the TV programme *Fawlty Towers*, John Cleese's Basil Fawlty is a prime example of a person who constantly struggles, and hilariously fails, to maintain his inner stability and keep life under control, and we love to see him, because we all know what it feels like.

When Inner Parents and Inner Children Get Together

An intimate relationship is an enormous threat to the precarious inner balance we have been describing. Within the fearful psyche intimacy is as dangerous as Kryptonite to Superman, for you cannot have a satisfactory relationship without both partners allowing themselves to be vulnerable and dependent together. But it is not so straightforward. Let us consider what happens when individuals come together. Imagine the interaction between four competing poles – or six, if you add on the adults they are intending to be. Relationship is a complex business!

In times of stress – and relationships can easily become stressful – the inner situation is heavily taxed. First we may try charm or manipulation; in other words, we may act from the child within us, while looking for a response from the parent part in the other. If that fails, we have recourse to our parent part, in which case we will be looking towards the child part in the other. In the long run, relationships can crystallize around such tendencies, so that partners find themselves unable to operate outside these restrictions. Each partner is unconsciously bonded from the position of their inner child with the hoped-for ideal parent which they see in the other. At the same time, the same-gender parent's attitude and behavioural tendencies towards the opposite sex are crucial in forming a base pattern for our own behaviour. These reinforce the inner parent and in consequence affect how we relate to our partners.

We call the patterns of interaction between the inner parts 'bonding patterns', a term first coined by therapists Hal Stone and Sidra Winkleman.[5] A chief feature of the bonding patterns we noticed in our own lives and those our client couples have told us about is the rapidity and predictability of the patterns and interactions. It's astonishing! In the case of our couple, the time that elapsed between the man wanting to make love and stomping off down the corridor was only a few minutes. Perhaps you recognize this speed in your own arguments, which, if you take the trouble to analyse them, usually turn out to be bonding pattern interactions. How do they get out of hand so quickly and where does this energy come from?

Bonding patterns are driven by the impulse to protect actual (or imagined) vulnerability, strengthened by the old adage that attack is the best form of defence. If you look closely at the dynamics in the example you will notice that there is a progressive but rapid escalation of hostility in each partner. Although this creates a lot of energy between the partners, it leads only to an impasse followed by separateness. And when they experience themselves as separate they do not have to be dependent on each other at all. Comforting togetherness has been lost, but a comforting independence has been gained.

However, as we saw in the previous chapter, such independence is more likely to be a compensation for the inability to be alone. It is driven by the inner child. Seen in this light, the distancing partner is still pushing for togetherness, but one marked by the closeness of conflict.

Bonding Patterns and the War in the Bedroom

If we could look inside the psyches of the couple in our story, we would witness a drama which evokes familiar disappointments and self-protection urges from their past. Here's how it works.

When the man experiences rejection from his mate he is most likely to experience a phantom from the past, a mother figure who at that moment is withholding what he desires. He feels rejected, fragile and vulnerable. In his unconscious mind, his wife is the one who is 'selfish', because she is bent on her own agenda, rather than focused on the needs of 'her child'. Whenever an ancient unavowed neediness creeps into sex you can be sure that a parent/child dynamic is being evoked, and that there will be trouble.

The man's sulky complaint comes from the wheedling little boy inside him and is designed to make the woman feel guilty for not taking care of him. It is aimed at a little girl in her, who he knows grew up feeling that she had to take care of everyone's needs. But it evokes an exasperated parent part in her. 'What *is* the problem?' is directed at the 'silly little boy' in the man. It is both a defence of her little girl, whom he was evoking, and a redirection of the action towards the area where she knows he hurts: the little boy who is prone to rejection. It is therefore both self-protection and counter-attack. But it is so innocent, and so rapid. And the reality is that the woman is probably motivated solely by a desire to protect her little girl from the inference that she is a *bad* girl for having failed to do what she was supposed to do.

To counter his feelings of rejection, the man first tries to manipulate the woman from his child place. 'I see I'm in the way,' he says innocently. As this seems to fail, he sees he has to get tougher to protect himself. So he escalates into his parent part. In this case it is an aloof and rather patronizing parent. 'I think you've got a real problem with sexuality' is fairly hostile. You don't have to get violent (though it does happen) in order to escalate; a falsely powerful superiority can be achieved by gestures and vocal tone. Some, especially the English, can achieve it expertly simply by raising an eyebrow. The point is that the escalation forces the energy in the opposite direction, since the invocation of the parent part is matched by aiming at the inner child in the partner.

The icy, aloof father threatens to withdraw, but his behaviour is also rather punishing, showing that he has not given up fishing for this bad little girl. He employs some of the style of a domineering, punishing father-who-is-to-be-obeyed. Could it be that she did in fact have a father who withdrew and abandoned her, or who was dominant and punishing? If so, then in this guise he is aiming directly for the little one in her, whose history he either knows or senses. Or could it be that his father was distant and aloof, and that this is an old identity pattern into which he slips in times of stress? It may even be a combination of both. Under the spell of a bonding pattern, in attack-in-order-to-defend mode, we intuitively seek out the particular kind of child that our partners were and supply them with the 'right kind' of parent to frighten them. And we know all these quite well, for when we fell in love we had a precise match between these inner figures.

But it is even more complex because our responses are partly modelled on those we learned from our parents. For example, the woman feeling the paternal hostility to her inner child has recourse to her inner parent for the express purpose of self-protection. But she is also influenced by the ways her mother reacted to her father or other males in her life. And in her own counter-offence towards her partner's child, she may be unknowingly influenced by the kind of attitudes which her mother had towards whiney, needy children. This in turn will be based on how her mother was mothered and therefore her mother's attitude to her own inner child. This will have profoundly influenced how the daughter was brought up, particularly what was allowable in terms of vulnerability and needs. These themes can go back generations. It is a veritable hall of mirrors! But for now, back to the action.

In response to her husband's further escalation the woman replies with venom: 'All you want is a mother to take care of your every little whim. Well, this lady ain't your mother, get it? Even if the last one was.' She has become a furious mother-figure, exasperated by the self-centred needy infant that it has been her unending misfortune to be stuck with. Give her strength!

In return, he has to escalate again, now turning into the ultimate know-it-all patriarch and putting his finger on her self-evident frigid pathology. How else can she now protect her 'useless' little girl but by becoming Jezebel the Merciless and dismissing him with one shake of her tail. And so he rides off into the icy sunset. A different type of man, with a different history, might have become Mr See if I Care I Can Rise above It All, or Conan the Barbarian, breaker of plates, vases and doors, while another woman might have escalated to Kali the All-Terrible, goddess of destruction, eater of male inner children!

And all in the name of protection of vulnerability. And all in a few minutes flat.

Bonding Patterns for Peace

Like all things in nature, bonding patterns come in countless varieties. A bonding pattern argument may be triggered at any time and be of any intensity. Couples at our workshops hearing about bonding patterns for the first time enthusiastically tell us about incidents from their daily lives which fit the structure. Often they have experienced one on the way to the workshop. Map-reading on a car journey is a sure-fire starting-point for many couples. Here, in a stereotypical case, the controlling father (primed by an anxious little boy) may exercise his infuriating influence on the 'useless little girl-woman'. Ordering in a restaurant or dealing with tradesmen or taxi drivers are other instances which frequently evoke bonding patterns. Partners seem to fall blindly into traps where they adopt a style – perhaps an angry mother or a critical father – quite without any intention that they themselves can recognize.

The bonding pattern of the couple we have been analysing is a dynamic one – it is all action. But there are many other varieties. Imagine the scenario with a different woman, one who is afraid of any conflict, or of upsetting the good father she has married. Perhaps she would have put down her book, become a compliant child and given to the little boy in the man what he needed to feel good again, without self-interest, but also without passion or desire.

There are many relationships which settle for the quiet life with inner children appeasing inner parents, afraid to rock the boat, settling for the known. These static bonding patterns serve to avoid conflict, to maintain the security of the pairings, based on the stable patterning of inner parent with inner child. Other patterns which appear dynamic are so repetitive that they create their own stability and are therefore also counted as static. These have their energy focused in only one direction, like the comic character Andy Capp, the cheeky child eternally meeting or outwitting the restrictive mother in his wife Flo. And then there are those where both partners collude in remaining children together, brother and sister, like the Babes in the Wood.

As society becomes more complex so do the roles and bonding patterns we find. Sometimes it is hard to spot when an apparently adult response is simply a pseudo-adult one. A pseudo-adult response is one in which the energy has gone from the child part to the parent part. It is not always an explicitly aggressive escalation, but it is defensively and strategically directed nevertheless. Such a move can be infuriating for the other partner, because it appears so innocent. But the experience of being on the receiving end is of an aggression so passive yet so finely tuned to making the other impotent that they become furious. Relationships can develop long-term patterning around such dynamics. For example, a 'new man' who has read all the right books can say all the right stuff. But if he is motivated by his inner child's fear of not upsetting mother, he can cause his partner to become so exasperated that she becomes the one who is 'carrying all the anger' on behalf of the relationship.

Although they do not feel particularly pleasant, dynamic bonding patterns have one advantage over static ones: mutually collusive patterns are harder to get out of than ones where partners collide with each other. In terms of transformative potential, the man in our example is extremely lucky to have a wife who is able to stand up to him. It can be considered a gift. For if at some point he bothers to take the time to think about what is going on, he will realize that he has to come to terms with what feeling rejected does to him. He will then begin to recognize to what lengths he will tend to go in order to prevent himself feeling his vulnerability. He will begin to see how he treats his own neediness. In short, he will be forced to look in the mirror that his partner offers him, through her refusal to comply with the demands of his needy inner child. If he then bothers to do the necessary psychological work he can come through it chastened and transformed. Then everything may change: his partner will feel much more secure around him and he may find that he begins to get much more of what he is longing for!

On the other hand, a relationship where both are doing all they can for stability or a quiet life – even if under the guise of 'not upsetting the children' – will more often than not turn out to be a static prison where there is no passion and no opportunity for growth. If there is any sex life at all, it is unlikely to mature and develop, and is more likely to wither and die. Over the years, any sense of shared intimacy will probably elude the couple. The woman who offers duty sex (or 'womb sex' as we call it) in exchange for peace is most likely to be stuck in a dutiful daughter or pacifying mother role. Her ability to obtain deep pleasure from this is doubtful. It may be difficult for her to surrender to her own orgasm and her health may well suffer. A man who is fully occupied with deploying his pleasing son role in his sex life may learn some useful techniques, but he will never penetrate the heart of his adult partner. If he remains in the old paradigm of 'giving her one' and rolling over, he will be sure to miss her altogether. In lonely complicity they may both settle for either of these patterns, but the man may find his own erective potency elusive in the long run.

Such a survival-bonded relationship may last a long time – many marriages have been based on such sound pragmatism – but the opportunities for growth will be stifled.

What is extraordinary about bonding patterns is how stable and enduring they can be. Even the most violent and abusive patterns are hard to break for this reason. Most battered wives, for example, go back home. Most psychologically castrated husbands stick around. The tacit refusal of both partners to look in the mirror of awareness means that they have agreed to put their priorities elsewhere. They may be able to maintain a stable relationship, what we call a 'maintenance marriage'. But if one partner wants things to change, then they will either have to get out or bring in a third party, by having an affair, for example.

For the bonds which characterize a maintenance marriage will need to be burst if a relationship is to grow into its true potential and go beyond self-betrayal for the sake of security.

CHAPTER 8

Self-Betrayal
in the Name of Love

He dreamed of
an open window.
A Vagina, said
his psychiatrist.
Your divorce, said
his mistress.
Suicide, said
an ominous voice within him.
It means you should close the window
or you'll catch cold, said
his mother.
His wife said
nothing.
He dared not tell her
such a
dangerous dream.

Felix Pollak[1]

'Why can't I be like other women and just do it so we can have peace?' she sighed to herself, feeling the heavy pressure in her heart. She had wanted to read, but realized that now she couldn't keep her *focus on the book. She was struggling to hold her tears back.*

Then she got furious. 'He's so selfish. Whenever he doesn't get what he wants, he sulks. Who wants to make love to that?'

Then she became sad again. 'Why can't he just stay and enjoy the feelings of closeness between us? Then I might become more interested in him than in the book. Or even if I continued to read, we'd be feeling close to each other, instead of this nightmare! Now I don't feel like making love to him ever again.'

Angry again: 'It has nothing to do with love anyway, he's just a stupid, spoiled brat, wanting mummy to prove he's a big man. I hate him!'

Crying now: 'It's not fair that he puts me through this, I don't deserve it! All I wanted to do was read. Just because I don't always want to make love when he does, it doesn't mean that I don't love him.'

Anger returns: 'If he was a real man he wouldn't want me to make love just to pacify him. That has nothing to do with real passion.'

Then a softening: 'I don't want it to be like this. I miss him, but I won't let him treat me like this.'

If we were able to eavesdrop on her internal dialogue into the wee hours, we would witness her constant oscillation between deciding to leave next morning to start a new life without him, wishing he were dead, wishing she were dead, seeing him as a monster and seeing herself as useless and wrong. She would occasionally wonder if he were also still awake and perhaps even hope that he would come back to bed. That would be nice. (There's a slight possibility however, that if he did come back, she would pretend to be asleep, or at least not show him how relieved and glad she was.) Perhaps she would wonder how he would receive her, if she went to him. Would she be compelled to make love to him to reassure him (or herself) of their bond? Would she want to? Could she?

On that particular night, escaping into unconsciousness, she eventually fell into an exhausted sleep. On other occasions she had gone to him, vulnerable and fearful, yet intending to open her heart to him and make up.

He too had been lying awake in the dark, busy with his own (not dissimilar) inner dialogue, also sad, fearful and lonely. But when he heard her approaching, he protected the longing in his heart, holding his breath and tightening the muscles in his chest. He had learned long ago to hold back his tears, especially when he was really sad. Showing his vulnerability had never brought him anything but more pain.

On other nights he came back, accepting her wish not to make love but wanting to be close to her warm body and be reassured that she still loved him. A part of him knew he wasn't perfect; in fact could be quite horrible sometimes. So he would risk returning to the joint bed with the tentative hope that she would understand and forgive. But he was wary. For some reason, the woman about to come through the door had the power to make him feel more vulnerable than anybody else he had ever met. So better beware. He stiffened.

As soon as she saw the cold look in his eyes and heard his disapproving voice say: 'What do you want?', she exploded inside.

Her inner parent warned her: 'You can either be close and dependent, or disconnected and independent – you can't be both!' And she knew how a woman could love too much and let herself be used by a man's emotional power games – history was full of it – so she wasn't about to let him get away with it. She was a modern, intelligent, professional woman and this old-fashioned stuff of women being there to please men when they wanted it was not for her. She was a free and independent woman, and if he couldn't face a real woman, it was about time he learned to! He needed to grow up!

He, for his part, was confronted by a coldness that came from generations back. It pierced him right through to some deeply buried memory of never feeling loved and wanted. His inner parent could hardly help him. He did not know how to deal with these women. To prevent himself from acknowledging the horrible feelings which the whole situation stirred up in him, he could only retaliate with as much dismissal and superiority that he could summon up from his ancestral coffers.

What was the same each time was that they'd be up most of the night, screaming or sneering at each other, alternating between outbursts of anger and blame, reproachful despair and terminal hopelessness. Then they would be back in their separate beds, without much rest. Both reactions were fuelled by wounds from long before they ever met. Neither was able to show their private inner vulnerability. They were still both protecting themselves against any new wounds in the best way they knew.

The following days were always difficult to face and even holidays often failed to offer any convincing solace.

Who needs love?

Is this process familiar to you? Or does it only happen to the neighbours? Perhaps you have your own specific version of the pain game? It doesn't have to be so active, or fuelled by sex, to create a deep, underlying rift between you.

For many couples the game stops here; they resign themselves to having grown apart over the years. Others progress to separation, thinking they're incompatible. Some decide they will never again expose themselves to being hurt and disappointed, and make sure that no one will ever come that close again. They can do that effectively even while staying in the relationship. It is easy to rationalize that this is just what happens in relationships and settle for the comfort that familiarity provides. Such couples busy themselves with children and jobs and accept the gap between them. You can make your own list of what fills up your gap: the TV, the computer, new projects, drink, drugs, affairs – whatever can be successfully employed to numb the nagging sense of loss and loneliness.

Sooner or later an intimate relationship will confront partners with the degree to which they prefer security to the risk of love. But it is nigh impossible to reconcile this dilemma without becoming aware of the forces at play beneath the interactions. If partners fail to solve this, a protest may well be made at some other level of the psyche. We suspect that anxiety, tension, depression, stress, addictions and phobias can be a result of such unrecognized internal conflicts. Long-term unhappiness may eventually present itself as physical symptoms or illness.

To build the picture further we need to investigate the subject of feelings. Feelings are the subject of most initial forays into the world of psychology, and many books. We do not want to reinvent the wheel; nevertheless, we must say a word or two here about feelings. To benefit from our engagement with the conflictual side of love, we will need to unlearn some outdated tricks from the past and learn some new ways of living with our emotions.

Living without Needs or Feelings

When we were children, we were sensitive and vulnerable to the people around us and to various degrees suffered at the hands of our caretakers. Even the most devoted and aware parents give their children cause to feel let down and betrayed. It is inevitable, because parents are ordinary, imperfect human beings. Furthermore, experiencing some disappointment is necessary for healthy psychological development. Psychologists call this 'providing optimum frustration'. This entails disappointing the children's needs enough to build tolerance of not having their needs met *instantly*, while meeting them *sufficiently* to prevent lasting damage to the fragile psyche. Throughout, the child needs to retain a sense of being cared about. In earlier generations, this latter qualification was frequently overridden, as babies were left to cry in their prams in order not to 'spoil' them. Clearly, it is no easy task to get the balance right, as all parents will appreciate.

It is safe to assume that most of us will have had some needs frustrated beyond our level of tolerance. If whenever we showed our discontent the outcome was that we were ignored or distracted, or (more seriously) punished, ridiculed, neglected or abandoned, then we eventually learned that it was better not to have certain feelings or needs at all. The problem is that they didn't just disappear because they weren't met. We had to *make* them disappear. The magic tricks at the child's disposal for achieving this are called repression and splitting. In other words, putting certain feelings in one box and 'me' in another. The more severe and frequent the frustration, the stronger the magic.

If we attempt to fit words to what goes on in a child's mind during this conjuring trick, they might run something like this:

I don't like it. I'm scared and I don't feel safe, and I'm a little angry. Actually I'm very angry, almost as angry as I am frightened. In fact, I'm so angry that I want to kill you!

Whoa! That's not safe. I can't survive without you and anyway you are stronger than me. So I'll kill the troublesome part of myself instead.

Now, that's better, do you like me now? Well, at least you are still here, so maybe if I get really good at this, you will like me so much that you will finally provide me with what I need.

By the way, I don't quite know what I need, but you do. So if I try really hard to become what you want me to be, will you look after me?

When children experience the gap between their needs and what is forthcoming, their only conceivable hope lies in convincing their caretakers that they are deserving. And so, when we are still very little, we learn that it is more productive to focus on skilfully manipulating the other than relying on our own feelings. Over time, as messages from our family of origin are overlaid with social and cultural norms, awareness of our original needs and feelings eventually fades into the background.

Depending on circumstances, the troublesome feelings and qualities which we may have little option but to drop will include anger, sexual arousal, excitement, playfulness, wilful assertion, sadness, fear, exuberance, joy, pride, vulnerability, confidence, trust, love, longing for independence, longing to belong and the need for acceptance or recognition. All these aspects are vital ingredients in adult relationships. But we have disowned them. They are not part of the selves we identify with. But our ability to be intimate or passionate in a sustained way is inevitably compromised, since all the aspects mentioned are vital ingredients in adult relationships. Instead, as 'lovers in training' we tend to run straight into disappointment and frustration.

Disappointment as the Great Awakener

When disappointment finally catches up with us in our adult relationships, we are faced with a problem. The experience of falling in love prises open the lid of the box where we dumped all that we disowned and our longings and hopes are stored in exactly the same box as our fear and anger. Now, with our unconscious control mechanisms less preoccupied with keeping the lid on, both the repressed fears and the repressed longings begin to reassert themselves. *And they are supposed to!* If we were not tricked into hauling back into consciousness all the anger and anguish stored up for so long, we might stay stuck in immature expectations of relationship based on manipulating the other. A part of us might settle for such a safe form of intimacy and develop it into co-dependency – the addiction to living as if the other were either the problem or the solution. But we have little hope of developing a more mature way of relating by resigning ourselves to a life of 'safe intimacy'. So relationships lovingly fool us into reviving our deepest hopes and fears, and though it may feel far from safe to do so, we are eventually rewarded if we dare to follow this prompting. This is one of the many blessings in disguise that we give each other in the dance of relationship. Not that it feels like a gift at the time – mostly it feels as if we have been cheated.

However, the encounter with disappointment and the return of repressed emotions presents us with a new choice, one which is more risky. Whereas as children we survived by repression, now we stand no chance of reaching true adult intimacy by continuing to run away from ourselves. In the film *Shadowlands*, the C. S. Lewis character describes the process perfectly when he says:

As a child I chose safety; as an adult I choose suffering.

This is not some appeal to the value of masochism, but a pointer towards becoming a more whole person. It suggests a shift from letting the child we were run our show to taking up an adult position – even if that is more difficult to manage and causes us to feel more vulnerable. Children have no real choice but to survive. As adults we can choose to live.

Betraying Autonomy or Betraying Love

By the time we are adults and in charge of our own choices about how we live, we enter a different context for self-care. Whenever we give another person the responsibility for our well-being we betray our autonomy. Likewise, if we choose to get out of a relationship just because it isn't fun anymore, we betray our heart, and with it our hopes of being loved and learning to love. However, assuming responsibility for ourselves is not easy. It is not a matter of heroic independence, nor of mastering the environment by manipulation. So where do we start?

The first step is to recognize how we maintain the trap in which we avoid taking responsibility. Unless we know where we are, it's difficult to decide how to get to where we want to be.

There is a model of self-betrayal frequently employed by counsellors called the drama triangle, or the victim, rescuer and persecutor syndrome, which can help us here. As a map of the dynamics of co-dependency, it offers a way of seeing which can be applied to all relational issues. The model suggests that it is easy to get stuck in patterns of unhealthy interaction with each partner constantly and helplessly alternating roles which act out a particular relational style.

We find that this model can be usefully applied to intimate relationships because its relatively simple formulation illus-

The Drama Triangle

Victim

Rescuer   Persecutor

trates the complex changes of roles within relationships where nothing ever really alters. Its triangular form is a mirror of the base from which every human being emerges: mother/father/child, otherwise known as the Oedipal triangle.

Depending on our experiences of our original triangle, we will be more at ease with one position than another, or more identified with a particular role than its alternatives. Most of us can probably spot how we opt for one or other role when the going gets tough in our relationships. The dynamics described by the drama triangle kick in automatically under stress and we invest our energy in many variations on a theme. The fascinating aspect of this troublesome triangle is the creativity it encourages in us.

We will now explore some possible scenarios. See whether these generalized examples ring any bells.

The Rescuer

Let us imagine that when you were young, someone else's needs were always more important than yours, so that you learned that it was not a good idea for you to be dependent and have needs. That somebody could have been a sibling, or a parent who was unable to cope with their physical or emotional disabilities, or to limit their selfish tendencies. Perhaps your parents were unhappy together and the insecurity fostered an atmosphere in which you felt responsible for their unhappiness

– whether they stayed together 'for the children' or not. All children want their parents to be happy and will do almost anything to achieve it. Under such adverse conditions, you learned not to expect others to be there to guide and support you. You had to become a premature little adult, adopting a role that was more like a parent than a child. You probably became very good at it!

This will have determined your blueprint for intimacy. You are used to providing love and care, so as an adult, you will most likely find yourself a partner who is not very good at loving and whose stance turns out to be more like that of a victim. Such a partner can furnish you with ample opportunity to supply devotion to their dependent, vulnerable side – which is the obvious way for you to show love and affection.

However, if you resonate with the role of rescuer, it is likely that a part of you is so used to not having your needs met that when your relationship runs into trouble – as it will – you attempt to maintain the status quo and salvage whatever possible, with little regard to your own needs or limitations. Your partner probably takes this for granted and expects that you can handle anything. But in the long run it depletes you and leaves you feeling empty.

Things are further complicated by your difficulty in asking for what you want – if you even know what that is. You find it hard to acknowledge that you are depleted and that you long to be cared for in return. After all, your wish to satisfy your partner's needs originated in the secret belief that you would eventually get *your* needs met by giving others precisely what you wanted for yourself. In this way, you unwittingly chose to forego your own needs, but sooner or later, whether you acknowledge it or not, you become full of resentment, which if not listened to may manifest as depression or illness. In the meantime, you find yourself turning into a smothering martyr, a nagging ogre or a sarcastic withdrawer.

A further possibility is that having been a rescuer in child-hood, you look for a relationship where you can be the one who is cared for, only to find that your partner was specifically attracted to the rescuer in you. If you are now no longer giving, you are perceived as a withholding and therefore *persecuting* figure. Whichever route you take, you now find yourself trapped in ways of behaving which betray not only your sensitivity and longing to share love, but also your genuine strength and competence.

The Victim

Whereas rescuers had to become little adults to foster the hope of being loved, those prone to the victim stance will have learned that staying dependent and needy was more likely to encourage a caring attitude. There are many variations of family situation which can generate the tendency to become a victim. In general, parents were either neglectful or persecutory, sometimes in extremely subtle ways. Moves towards independence or assertion, not to mention angry outbursts, were likely to have been met with disapproval, and therefore interpreted as threats to the hope of being loved.

Such threats can take the form of emotional blackmail. Perhaps a parent installed a sense of guilt in the child for no longer needing them or, for example in the case of an only child, the incentive was to be a special success just for them. The only way such a child can win on its own terms is by failing. A subtle variation is granting the child independence without regard to its limitations, thus ensuring failure and a return to dependency. 'See, you can't do without me' is the message.

If love was granted on condition of not being allowed to express *genuine* vulnerability or assertion, you are unlikely to have learned how to manage your needs or feelings. You may exhibit much emotionality, with a neediness you cannot contain, or alternatively, you funnel your feelings into some addiction. Your fall-back position is 'poor little me'. You seek a love which is a surrender of responsibility to the other. You will most likely choose a partner who learned to give up their own needs and is a rescuer. Conveniently, your partner's strategy of not having feelings or needs and yours of not taking any responsibility for them make a perfect fit. Perfect, of course, as long as your partner doesn't drop their rescuer stance! When they conclude that you will *never* grow up and start to feel *victimized by you*, the sparks are likely to fly.

If, on the other hand, your partner is more prone to the persecutor role, it can become really painful. The price of staying in a childish position with such a partner is high. There is little outlet for self-expression, since this means losing dependence and therefore 'lovability'. Since the only known and permissible source of personal power is using your skills to manipulate others, sooner or later you risk turning into a persecutor yourself – not only to yourself, but to anybody who loves you.

The Persecutor

The key to understanding the persecutor is that there is usually a victim hiding behind this relational style. Like the victim, the person driven to act in persecutor style is most likely to have been neglected or kept overly dependent, a child who was never allowed to become powerful. But the prohibition on neediness and the role-model of powerful uncaring adults will have encouraged the development of a detached and pseudo self-sufficiency.

Whereas traits of the first two types are relatively easy for most of us to identify with, acknowledging the persecutor in oneself can be more difficult. After all, there is something endearing in a person who wants to help others, and a person who suffers *does* elicit a degree of care, however irritating they can be. But none of us wants to be recognized as a persecutor.

Persecutors are not always loud and angry, nor overtly violent – though they can be. Often their style may be to employ demeaning little comments, innocently cruel behaviour or a consistent undermining of anyone who shows vulnerable or loving feelings. They can be masters of the water-drip torture, so expert that no single comment or action justifies the partner's growing despair. If they are challenged, they complain that *you* are persecuting *them* – they meant no harm, it was only a joke! The partner who is victim to a persecutor can feel that they are going mad. In fact, when unchecked, such actions, comments and attitudes create fear, mistrust and hurt, and can seriously damage the partner.

Persecutors are attracted to both rescuers and victims and they know how to deal with anyone who complains. Accusations that their behaviour is not justifiable are guaranteed to escalate a persecutor's defence. After all, they have to put up with the 'impossible' other's 'uselessness' or 'over-sensitivity'! The difficulty is that persecutors do not think they are doing harm. They tend to experience themselves mainly as long-suffering victims and sometimes as martyred rescuers – or both at the same time. There is some truth in this, for behind every bully hides a frightened soul. Persecutors secretly experience themselves as powerless and helpless.

If you are prone to this stance, you may have originally concluded that identifying with strength was your only available means not to be destroyed by a tyrannical parent or by overwhelming social pressures, such as losing your home too early. You were raised to be self-reliant and logical. Situations involving irrationality, vulnerability, sensitivity or feelings of love risk undermining your emotional survival. Your blueprint for loving relationships is steeped in fear and mistrust, and you protect your longing heart with barbed wire. In order to maintain a self-image of one who is powerful and in control – not at the mercy of others – you now apply the same treatment which you suffered to others' vulnerability and sensitivity. Nevertheless, you are quite good at making sure you get what you want. In time, the people who love you end up feeling more powerless and helpless than you, while you maintain the illusion of yourself as a capable or caring person, sacrificing yourself for others' benefit.

One who is well rehearsed in the role of victim will be the perfect partner for you, so that you keep your cover. If you find yourself with a rescuer, however, your self-assured demeanour is likely to have been a major attraction – you are someone they finally would not have to look after. But with a rescuer's fine-tuning for taking responsibility for others and not having their own needs met, your partner will have sniffed out your despair and put on their shining armour, ready to save you from yourself. You are likely to have spent a lot of energy fighting against this, since revealing a need to be saved would give away *your* inner secret. In their longing to be loved by you, all their time and energy is focused on you. Endlessly guessing what could please, they live for the occasional glimpse of sweet light escaping the shutters on your heart.

After some years, they may resort to complaints or pleas, but these only give you scope for showing your superior innocence and patience in dealing with this increasingly pathetic creature. If your partner stays, all the helplessness and vulnerability that you don't know how to deal with in yourself will be neatly located in the other. Your unconscious aim of rendering your partner more helpless than you may well be achievable, but as this happens, you are likely to lose interest in the relationship. Their obvious weakness and helplessness may also frighten you. Eventually, having successfully made your partner a victim, you may long to be with someone who is your equal. But if you leave for another you have to start all over again, training a partner to carry and express your vulnerable side. If you stay, every day is a reminder of your self-betrayal. You are a prisoner in your own trap.

If your rescuer wakes up from their trance, you will feel their reproach, and when you feel helpless, you will want to split up and put your rescuer back into the victim position. But if they are determined enough, you will overtly become their project. Now they demand that you work hard to recover your long-lost vulnerability and try to develop an ability to love. In this case, you may feel that you will never learn it fast enough for the lover who now appears to have become *your* persecutor.

Dancing a Three-Step Shuffle

In the above, you may have noticed how each role dovetails with the others. In time, rescuers are destined to turn into either victims or persecutors – there is no other option, since rescuing is a compensated position. Deep down, they are victims, since they do not know how to prioritize their own needs directly. The victim's power to make others feel guilty or responsible can at times seem more reminiscent of a persecutor, while a person strongly anchored in the persecutor's role can be seen as an amalgamation of victim and rescuer. The persecutory aspects stem from not really knowing how to care about another. Their need not to seem like a victim but to appear as one who is always in control means that they are constantly preoccupied with rescuing themselves. And on it goes.

These roles do not mean that we have no genuine ability to either care, suffer or take charge of our lives. But they do mean that all our emotional resources are needed in situations where we experience the need to *protect* ourselves or *control* the other. A relationship can give plenty of scope for that, but this cannot take the couple towards intimacy. Like the Pushme-Pullyou and the bonding patterns it is a game which can be played for evermore. The only way out is to get to *the heart of the matter*.

The first step towards this is recognizing how we hurt our lover. This certainly means recognizing the feelings repressed in the past and understanding how we constructed our compensated self-images, as well as acknowledging the roles which we gravitate towards in order to manipulate the other, fuelled by our belief that our needs will never be met otherwise. The ways we struggle to manage the precarious balance of power and vulnerability will need to be revised.

It may seem impossible to reconcile power and vulnerability, for they appear to be forces at opposite poles. Yet this reconciliation is exactly what is needed if we are serious about becoming *intimate adult* partners.

PART 3

In the Mud of Eden

CHAPTER 9
Vive la Diffrence!

I wanted one life
you wanted another
we couldn't have our cake
so we ate eachother.

Roger McGough[1]

When they heard the sound of car wheels crunching on the gravel they both heaved a secret sigh of relief. In fact, they were equally delighted no longer to be alone. But they did not share this with each other. For that would have seemed unkind. They moved slowly towards their guests, who were getting out of the car, smiling and stretching after their long journey.

'Wow, this is great!' said the male visitor, looking around him and taking his hostess in his arms for a big hug and a kiss.

'Shall I show you around? Or would you like to have a drink first, you must be tired after all that driving?' she offered.

'No, let's take a look, don't you think, sweetheart?' he answered, turning to his wife. 'Brilliant place you found us, I'm dying to see it all.'

So all four set off into the garden of the holiday cottage, past the rose trellis and over the little stream where they could make out

127

the rest of the village, huddled together in a delightful old-fashioned way.

They had been there for a couple of weeks already and had seen no one but each other during that time. So the arrival of their friends for the final week of their holiday was a big event. Already her office and his common-room seemed miles away, in a different life. They were both strangely missing something about their working lives. Surely it was not the activity, for they both found the peace of the countryside a fabulous balm. But there was something lacking.

'Great to see you,' said the male host to his friend, meaning it although he did not really know why it was, nor how to follow this statement up. But he was aware that the newly arrived shot of maleness had a powerful effect on him. So they walked almost in silence, some four or five paces behind the women, who were already chatting amiably, quite without looking at the scenery, or so it seemed to him.

When they had completed their tour and found themselves back in the yard, all four were together again, facing each other. Somehow, their faces had relaxed. They seemed more content.

'Come on, let's all have a drink,' he said, putting his arm warmly round his wife.

'And something to eat,' she added, moving into his embrace and beaming at their guests. 'You must be starving.'

The Problem of Difference

Difference is a difficult subject for human beings. The ability to hold paradox and to accommodate difference is an extremely sophisticated achievement of the human mind. Nevertheless, it is an art well worth learning if on a global level we want to put an end to social oppression, scapegoating, wars, ethnic cleansing, and so on.

Nowhere is this issue of difference more immediately apparent than right back home in our own relationships. So far we have been observing how couples start off in a dream of unconditional love and are then rudely awakened by repulsion caused by the awareness of difference they become locked in bonding patterns, projecting and mirror dancing, struggling with those aspects of difference for which they cannot not find a tolerable balance.

Whenever we experience difference that we cannot accommodate, we polarize. This catapults us into an energetic field where our sense of self is threatened. The relationship may not survive if it seems a toss-up between 'my life' and 'this relationship'. Frequently we reason: 'No man/woman is worth this hell – I'm off.' Alternatively, if we are more timid, we keep the whole thing under wraps and leave it to the next generation to sort out.

So far we have seen that the chief relationship problems involve the tension between separateness and togetherness and the polarizations between power and vulnerability and between disowned parts of our inner family. We have noticed that into these arenas come all our past mind-sets, our unconscious limitations and qualities, our dreams of the perfect parents. Paradoxically, these polarizations give us the opportunity to become aware of all the compromises we have made in the past for the sake of security and all the familial issues that are yet to be completed. But now we come upon the third great area of polarization, and this is one that is not personal – it is archetypal, or universal. It is the polarization of gender difference – the most basic equation of the man/woman relationship.

Gender Psychology and Imagination

'Everything is born of Woman' runs a Native American proverb. In the 1950s, from within his laboratories, Professor Alfred Jost made the shattering revelation that:

> The natural form of the human is the female; a male is the result of interference with 'natural' female development.[2]

Inside the human womb each egg always bears a particular chromosome, known as X. When an egg is fertilized by a sperm carrying the same kind of chromosome, a female foetus is produced – a double X. Before she is born, this little girl has already gained some measure of completion, for in her ovaries she possesses all the eggs she will ever need in her whole life. But to produce a male, a series of tentative manoeuvres will have to succeed. If a sperm carrying the other type of chromosome (the so-called Y) strikes lucky, then eventually, if everything goes according to plan, a male foetus is the result – an XY.

Becoming a male, therefore, implies an interference with the 'natural' route. In the early days of development, deep inside the womb, the foetus starts to grow, implacably female. After a few weeks, if the Y chromosome is present, it informs the gonads that they are destined to become testicles. But in order to stay male this foetus has to produce many hundreds of hormonal secretions and actions so as not to continue as a female, which is nature's base position, or it loses its line of masculine differentiation and reverts. The first action of the famous hormone testosterone is to fight off femininity. Edward Goldwyn, writer of a BBC *Horizon* programme, *The Fight to be Male*, explains:

> The testicles do not sit there passively, but first pump out a hormone which actively absorbs the female parts that would otherwise become the womb. Then they produce the major male hormone – testosterone – which stops the male parts degenerating.[3]

This extraordinary story of the origins of our life leads us to imagine that when the male foetus finally emerges he must be worn out, exhausted and distrustful of the feminine. We do not know whether he yet feels sorry for himself. Can we attribute the characteristic male restlessness to his intrauterine life? As soon as he is born, he looks to his mother's arms for comfort, as he may well continue to do in one form or other throughout his life. But he is in for more problems, for by the time he has developed his mental and physical faculties enough to be ready to tackle the dilemma of sameness and difference, he is in for a big shock.

Girls and boys, as they awaken to gender, will have a different experience as they recognize either their essential difference or their essential similarity to mother. For a boy, the experience of difference from mother is a major formative step. This process has been studied by Liam Hudson and Bernadine Jacot, husband and wife researchers from the Institute of Human Relations at the Tavistock Clinic. Following the psychoanalyst Greenson, they suggest that in order to get their identity needs met, boys have, as it were, to leave mother and find their fathers.[4] They must achieve a psychological separation from mother and 'counter-identify' with their same gender parent. If father is not present, due to physical or energetic absence from the home, or does not provide a satisfactory role model for the boy – for example if he is violent – then the boy is placed in limbo in relation to finding his gender identity. Hudson and Jacot argue that this early experience of difference and need to counter-identify becomes 'an enduring sense of dislocation' and constitutes an essential and existential wound, which they call 'the male Wound'.[5]

The girl, on the other hand, becomes aware that she *is* the same as mother. And this is *her* problem. She will have to look to father to get her earliest relationship needs met, but the sameness as mother can have the effect of preventing the development of a healthy independent sense of self. We have frequently heard from adult women in therapy how they have spent their lives not really sure that they exist. This can come as a shock to a male therapist, who is unlikely to be familiar with this issue from the inside. Females do not have the same kind of wound as males, nor the same kind of existential journey to make. They have their own wounds and their own individuation to deal with.

The daughter's 'female wound' appears to be more about getting some 'psychic space' from mother and a sense of autonomous valued existence. This can be compounded by the fact that she often has to look to the father for this, since her own gender has had few socio-political associations of power. To complicate matters, when the daughter's wound is passed on down from the mother, a girl can find it hard to receive the impression that she is a being of worth.

Drawing on studies from psychoanalysis and art, Hudson and Jacot propose that these similarity-and-difference experiences have an effect on the imaginative faculty of men and women. By 'imagination' they mean 'the mind's central function', that which influences all tendencies to conceptualize and act. The effect of both the male and female wounds, they say, is to create – in greater or lesser degrees – a tendency to think or act in particular ways. In times of stress, or when individuals are uninterested in becoming aware of their actions, these tendencies become aggravated and can become pathological.

In a male these will be a preponderance towards an insensitivity to others, a selfishness, a distrust of the opposite sex and objectivity, as well as a sense of agency, a tendency to treat people as if they were things, while personifying and loving things, ideals or technology. By this reasoning, much of the male's tendency for projects, thought, action, etc., is less to do with evolutionary drives (man the hunter), but, using the model we introduced in Chapter 6, more with having developed his *autonomy at the expense of his belonging needs*. The classical male imagination is then understandably suffused with a sense of distance or separateness. This imaginative tendency makes differentiation natural and relationship difficult.

So far, the result of this speculation is not much different from conclusions already drawn from common sense: men are not naturals at relationship – it is something they have to learn!

The girl, on the other hand, affected by the lack of dissimilarity to the mother, has to struggle to get some distance from her, often in an atmosphere of rivalry. Additionally, if the daughter's presence evokes the mother's envy, due to her own dissatisfaction with life, then the situation becomes more threatening to the girl's sense of autonomy. Moreover, because of the inherent ability to tune into another, which being able to give birth and nurture another being implies, the female psyche is naturally attuned to cross boundaries. A woman's imaginative world is essentially subjective, is the opposite of distanced – one could almost call it 'crowded'. Sometimes it is hard to know whose feelings are whose.

The continuing gender symbiosis with the mother produces ambivalence. As a result, reason Hudson and Jacot, though finely tuned in to the nuance of human sensitivity and relationship, the girl:

> ...will be more likely than her brothers to become preoccupied with issues of responsibility and blame. As she cannot express anger toward her mother without threatening her own identity, the small girl's anger will also translate itself into depression.[6]

Or, as Christiane Olivier, a feminist psychoanalyst, suggests, it will be expressed in body symptoms and eating disorders. We see this today in epidemic proportions, fanned by the relentless consumerism of fashion.[7]

If this analysis is correct, we have one explanation for gender differences which are not fully determined by culture. But on top of this, we have also to add in cultural and political issues.

Equality in Difference

The West has recently been experiencing a movement away from gender difference and towards making everyone the same. This can be viewed as an historical reaction to the political disadvantage of many groups: gender, racial and social. The so-called Women's Liberation Movement was a blast of fresh air which deeply disturbed the assumptions of the previous 200 years. Feminism still has a way to go in freeing women from social slavery and oppression across the globe, but it has radically altered our sense of how gender inequalities come to be taken as the norm.

Next, the new social sciences demonstrated how our language, unconscious expectations and cultural settings invariably tend to favour particular interest groups. We soon learned to be suspicious of all traditional roles and symbols in the gender arena. Sexual freedom and sexual choice for all became the banner cry raised against centuries of repression and we finally began to open up the sexual debate. This too still has a way to go to dispel widespread sexual ignorance. But now, in memory of how we felt stifled by the old-world attitudes, many of us deliberately try to live differently from the values associated with our own gender groups because they seem outmoded or unfair.

Lately, however, we are beginning to realize that we may have a new tyrant on our hands: extreme 'political correctness' may inhibit free thought as effectively as its rival, which, with all good intentions, it is busy replacing. As a society, we may well be in danger of ducking the issue of gender by failing to understand it. The differences clearly remain, however we deconstruct or politicize them.

Sometimes it can be enormously helpful to leave the influence of our own cultural setting to experience some of the value of those differences. As therapists, we visit other lands, eager to see how others experience the world of gender.

Whenever we have travelled in the indigenous world we have been struck by the clarity of gender roles and division. We emphasize that it is not our aim to romanticize or idealize other cultures. But we suspect that underlying traditional customs of indigenous communities, there may be some wisdom which the West has lost and is worth recovering, even when outward forms jar with our modern sensibilities.

In the villages in upper Gambia, for example, we noticed how the women were always doing some sort of work, while appearing to do it at a gentle pace, full of relational activity, chatting with their girlfriends, attending to the children, flirting with a passing male, seeming secure in their gender identity. Whenever they went to the well, it was women only. If a man ever approached he would be the subject of outrageous playful teasing from the combined force of the women.

In many indigenous societies the roles assigned to the genders seem to be connected to their archetypal symbolism. In the Atlas mountains of southern Morocco we saw how the women were constantly occupied with the maintenance work on the farms. They would cut fodder on the hillside and carry it home for the beasts. The men did their own work, which seemed mostly sporadic, and it was tempting to imagine that they were exploiting the women's labour. But when they applied themselves they worked with extraordinary concentration. This usually involved a project, a new construction, building a wall, undertaking an expedition. It was as if the women's work was circular and the men's linear.

With the Hopis in northern Arizona we noticed how the whole village turned out to prepare the land. All were involved with ploughing, harrowing and flooding the fields. But only the women were allowed to do the sowing. Only the women were deemed to be able to infuse the corn seeds with the creative capacity for giving birth to new life which the tribe knew to be the provenance of woman.

Even in southern France, when the old Occitan speakers harvest their grapes they celebrate with a fabulous lunch in a specially cleared barn. The men sit at one end of the table and the women at the other. The women serve the men, but they are not subservient. The men honour them for what they bring. After a while, as the wine flows, a delicious tension arises between the two groups. There is a flirting backwards and forwards, a teasing, a light but heady infectious energy that sweeps you up. At the end of the meal the women effortlessly clear the table, then sit together in the shade, chatting and laughing, occasionally glancing up towards the men and provoking them a little, while they are busy unloading the wagons of grapes into the crushing tank. It is profoundly juicy, soulful and sexual, and hardly anyone is under 65!

The point is that a secure gender identity is not only a force for social cohesion, but one which supplies an inner confidence which adds zest and prepares the ground for relationship and for whatever that may create. Relationship conflicts are often gender based and are always difficult, no matter where you are born. Belonging to a healthy gender group helps. For if we feel the support and resources of our own gender, we are more likely to have the courage to face the other and the interest to try to decode their language. Moreover, gender-focused rituals help to 'ground' men and women in their deeper natures. Without this connection it is difficult to express both masculine and feminine qualities with conviction.

Gender Group Support

An enhanced interest in a person's own gender group, and consequently in the opposite gender, is a reality which we have seen demonstrated time and time again in our workshops. Most couples who attend are new to the work and are understandably nervous about turning up to a workshop with their partner, even if they are workshop junkies on their own! You never know what your partner is going to say about you. There is palpable relief in the first hour when people realize that they are amongst an even number of their own gender in the room and that these people seem to be going through similar issues. They then recognize that some of these issues may not be as personal and unique to themselves as they had originally imagined. The value of normalizing this cannot be overestimated. In our introductory relationship workshops we have only one hour in separate gender groups, but the quality of presence is remarkable when the two sexes ceremonially come back together into the joint group.

There is both a huge wisdom and a common-sense principle here: if we know who we are and learn to take pride in our gender identity, we are then free to be curious about the other.

This curiosity is there, often yet untapped, despite our experiences. Witness the huge popularity of John Gray's books. He addresses something for which we have a deep hunger. However, despite the good things that undoubtedly are in Gray's books, we do not entirely endorse his approach. For us, it is not enough to learn the language and ways of the other in order to stay *out* of trouble. We believe that we are destined to get *into* trouble with the other gender and that only a firm gender identity, developing self-awareness and a creative attitude to life can help. Here we are more inclined to the view of storyteller Michael Meade:

Peace is not found by avoiding trouble, but by engaging it.[8]

CHAPTER 10

The Dance of Gender

Relationship is the yoga of the West.

Ram Dass

'But I didn't mean it to be criticism,' he said. 'I just don't think it works best like that.'

'Don't play the innocent with me,' she retorted. 'You've got that look and that tone just like your father.'

'Oh rubbish,' he snapped, turning away to face the garden.

'Don't run out on me now,' she continued. 'Have some courage, man. Can't you see that now you're in a bonding pattern, just like the one Nick and Helena spotted at the workshop?'

'More rubbish,' he stammered. 'If anyone's in one of those idiotic bonding patterns its you. Why are you stirring things up? What on earth do you want? Why don't you just take it easy?'

'What do I want? For a start I don't want you to talk to me like that. I don't want to be told I'm too emotional, or that I'm pre-menstrual or some such shit. I'd be delighted if you would take some responsibility for once and I'd appreciate it if you listened to me once in a while, like you promised the other night, but you clearly have no intention of carrying out your promise, it was all a load of bull as usual, so I might just as well be talking to myself.'

'Christ,' he muttered, under his breath, vaguely wishing that Simon and Louise were still here and he could get some support from his friend. He looked out towards the downs, barely visible beyond the village in the failing evening light. Leaving tomorrow. Back home. Back to work.

'See, you're not interested in listening at all. Are you? Where the hell are you? I bet you were thinking about going home and getting back to work on the extension again, weren't you?'

'No, as a matter of fact you're wrong,' he said defiantly, looking at his feet.

'Come on,' she said with a smile, 'you're guilty as anything. You're a hopeless liar, admit it!'

'If you must know, I was thinking about that new seminar I've got to give next week and how to approach it. I've done absolutely no preparation this holiday, what with everything that's been going on,' he added with a final hint of reproach.

'You'll soon be safely back at work, darling,' she said, with a long sigh of frustration that seemed as familiar to him as her very body. Then she walked back into the cottage and headed for the bathroom, leaving him standing gazing out into space, looking lost.

The ideas about gender which we proposed in the last chapter and those which follow are not meant to be the last word on the subject — but they do offer a direction, a starting-point for discussion. Unpacking the complexity would take a whole book to do the subject justice. The risks with all such gender arguments are of creating further stereotypes. But, in taking this risk, our hope is that each gender may be able to develop more understanding, empathy, and compassion for the other. We think that such understanding and compassion are needed.

The Male and Female Wounds in Relationship

In an intimate relationship the difficulties of each gender's imaginative tendencies and basic fears become exacerbated. And because these are different and complementary they will tend to jar and spiral into increasing levels of impasse.

Most important for us here is how each tends to regard the business of being in a relationship. For example, at a depth at which it is hard to fully appreciate, the man will expect his relationship with his woman to reconnect him to the source of love and stillness, and to be a respite from the busy and aggressive external world. This is natural given his experience of the male wound. However, he is likely to expect it to happen without much effort on his part.

Meanwhile, at a deep imaginative level, the woman looks to relationship as a chance for creativity, freedom and expression. But, since relationships involve men, who often need to be coaxed into learning its arts, all too frequently she ends up disappointed. Furthermore, she will need to find expression for a reservoir of dissatisfaction and frustration with both her own and the opposite gender, stemming from both the lack of freedom with the mother and the failure of the father to help her resolve this. Then there is her political gender inheritance! These demands will certainly frighten her spouse.

In direct complement to either gender's imaginative tendencies are their base level fears. The male's close relationship with separation begets his archetypal worst fear of *engulfment*. This terror of being overwhelmed, especially by the female, is perhaps a legacy of the intrauterine struggle we described earlier. It is easy to see how sometimes these fears can be projected out onto the female genitals and turn the longing for reconnection into the fear of sexual intimacy.

In contrast, the female's association with closeness is paired with her worst fear – that of *abandonment*, or being ignored, or being over-controlled. She will frequently betray herself to prevent these fears being actualized. Imagine how all this plays out in the daily life of the relationship.

This oversimplification inevitably hides a world of complexity. Add to this each person's unique family background and we open to unlimited variations on a theme. Later in this chapter we will explore why some men and women can experience those primary fears opposite to what we suggest as gender specific.

On top of this come the cultural problems. The personal is also the vehicle for the political, whether consciously felt or not, and whether we like it or not. Anger from centuries of male oppression over the female will come out, and will need to be heard and received by the other. Such things need to be received personally. It is perhaps unfair on the male, but there is no other way, while it still simmers inside the female and equality is still uncertain. But his lack of talent for relationship, his ineptitude at listening for long periods and his tendency to resolve situations by retreating to distance and separateness – what John Gray calls the use of his 'cave' – can make the situation seem hopeless.[1]

In an opposite scenario, a woman's relational interests and her own sense of authority may be trivialized in her current relationship. This may become a recreation of how things were at home when she was a little girl struggling for a sense of independent worth in the world of her mother. She may well resort to depression. Diagnosed depression is far more common in females than in males. However, men may not be much better off, as family therapist Ronald Taffel suggests:

The distinction between depression and the everyday state of many men is not so clear-cut. What should we call someone who does not feel very much, who has no real friendships, who has few interests other than work, and cannot relate to the people close at hand?[2]

Unless both men and women can find a way to acknowledge their imaginative trends and thereby go beyond those limits, they can become lost in the battle between the sexes.

And yet in their imagination there lies a solution too.

If the woman learns to *recognize her intrinsic wholeness*, as the female foetus so clearly displays, she can see that her path is towards accepting and embracing her femaleness, just as she is, independent of external affirmation.

If the man can recognize that he has to learn *to go beyond his imaginative default mechanism*, and that this is indeed a worthy project, he can enter his deeper male nature.

We say that there is a dance. It's a bit like a waltz – the woman needs to do 'the one-step' and the man 'the two-step'.

We are now ready to look further into the mechanics of this dance.

The Dance of Energy

The Tantric adepts of India and their counterparts in China, centuries ago, held that men and women could find harmony by directing and balancing the different *energetic* flows inside them. Sexual practices were one way of achieving this. We do not know much about these sages' beliefs about relationship, since the bulk of their teachings were secret. But we do know that men and women were regarded as equals *in their difference* and furthermore as each other's consorts. A consort in this sense is one who is a teacher who challenges and catalyses the partner. The religious art of Tibet beautifully illustrates this. Most paintings and sculptures feature a Buddha and his consort in a sexual position within a ring of fire.

In these teachings, gender difference and complementarity were derived from the body and its energetic centres. The energy wheels of the chakras, recently introduced to the West and popularized through yoga, was one way this knowledge was systemized. Yet the concept of the body having an energetic system has found little place in Western science. Here, the body is traditionally viewed as a mechanical vehicle, with the brain and its nervous system as driver. In consequence, most scientific studies of gender, outside the anthropological and evolutionary fields, have had to do with investigating brain size and hemispherical loci of control.

One piece of recent enquiry, however, promises to bring the non-Western science of energetics together with modern depth psychology. Dr Willem Poppeliers, working in the Netherlands, has come up with a new body psychotherapy theory which can explain much of what goes on between men and women. He calls it Sexual Grounding Therapy.

Human beings, according to Poppeliers, have three principal energetic centres: the head, the heart and the genitals. We have already made several suggestions about the mental and imaginative gender differences, and it is what Poppeliers has to say about the latter two which interest us most here. Each gender, he claims, has a different *priority of charge* in their heart and genitals. This affects the *internal* relationship between an individual's heart and genitals, as well as *external* relationships and thereby the interplay between the genders.

In this model, if we think of the human body as a conduit for an electric current, we can say that the female is *positively* charged in the heart and *negatively* charged in the genitals. The male has the opposite set-up. His genitals hold the positive charge and his heart the negative. In this way, each gender has an initial tendency to be undercharged or undeveloped in their negative poles and as a consequence to find life more difficult in these areas – that is, matters of the heart for the male and matters of the genitals for the female.

What does Poppelier's theory mean in practice, in terms of how we have seen this dance so far?

The heart is the seat of feelings and love, and the genitals of desire and power. The potential here is a wonderful fulfilling circular flow between the man and woman, due to the complementary nature of the initially charged centres. But in practice, there are huge difficulties because of each gender wanting to give, or lead with their positive pole and not wanting to receive with their negative pole.

A woman's familiarity with the energy of the heart, for example, means she can often end up literally forcing emotions down the throat of her emotionally timid man or busting her heart trying to change him into the emotionally available man she longs for. The man, on the other hand, may seek a genital connection as a prime means of establishing a flow or release of charge from his positively charged genital centre. He is likely to end up frustrated to find that his woman does not want to let him in until she feels that his heart is open to her. But opening up his heart for him means being vulnerable, since this is his undeveloped negatively-charged pole. He has little experience of what his inner flow may feel like and the demand from her brings him in touch with his prime fear of engulfment.

If this impasse is resolved by the woman giving way to him, while excluding her heart from their love-making, a joyless marriage is guaranteed. If she stands firm she will have to face her own worst primal fear, that of abandonment.

The Inner Balance of Masculine and Feminine

Poppeliers is entirely in tune with Hinduism and Taoism when he says that the primal energy is itself divided into *Receptive Creative* and *Active Penetrative*. These energies are present in both sexes: physically, they correspond to the nature of their genitals, for the vagina both receives and gives birth, whereas the penis is designed purely to inseminate. Psychologically, however, they may be expressed in a variety of ways: the way a person is able to let another affect them, for example, or is able to take their stand in the world.

Due to our history and gender identity issues, each one of us is likely to have a different relationship with these energies. For instance, a woman who is what Marion Woodman has called a 'father's daughter' – one who has decided that the male way offers more promise than the female – may have more penetrative energy available to her than a receptive, 'soft' or 'new' man.[3] He, in turn, may well be more receptively than penetratively oriented, since he has not found the father's way attractive enough to identify with, and turns to love and understanding as his basic approach to life. When such a pair live together they will polarize as much as any classic couple until they learn how together they can balance these energies.

The task of learning to regulate and balance these energies starts very early in life and varies according to the changing phases of life, says Poppeliers. Ideally, children would be taught by their parents, both directly and by example. However, the sexual ignorance in our culture usually precludes that. First, because for generations people have been unable to solve their Oedipal issues. In other words, as parents we have little skill at integrating our children into the sexual relational world of our intimate relationships, even though they are the direct consequence of our love-making. Secondly, Western society has had such a taboo on the genitals that it has had the effect of rendering them chronically over-excited in the population at large, reasons Poppeliers. In consequence, men and women have not achieved a balanced flow between their own heart and genitals.

The results of this are all too evident in gender relations and the worst case scenarios are very grim. Either a male is afraid of his positive charge and unable to stand firmly and be fully intimate and sexual or he may use his over-stimulated genital charge to objectify the opposite sex. In the worst case he may rape. Such an act represents his inability to imagine being able to enter a woman in any other way and his unacknowledged inner sense of powerlessness. In other words, a rapist cannot conceive that he can gain access to a woman's heart, so he does not try.

A woman who is unsure of her negative pole, her self-worth, her standing in the world, her sexual drive, may similarly overuse her heart and her emotions to abusive effect. Here the woman, hungry for the man's emotional openness and frustrated by his response, 'rapes' him in his heart, overwhelming him with rage, emotionality or seduction.

At the other end of the scale, however, if the awareness, regulation and balance of these energies become a priority for individuals, an extraordinary beauty can emerge.

The complementary nature of the energetic flows predict that men and women can come together gracefully. Their centres are complementary and attractive: the penis seeks the vagina, the vagina wants to embrace the penis; both hearts – which are the same and entirely equal – wish to connect. When men learn to inform their genital energy from a connected heart and women bring their vaginal power and authority into their loving, marvellous things can occur. The two energies alchemize.

Poppeliers suggests that the complete and balanced individual has imaginatively internalized a set of inner parents who are loving and sexual towards each other. This possibility, brought about through the harmonization of these energies, is available to all, he claims. This seems closely to resemble what Carl Jung called 'the inner marriage', the goal of individuation. In energetic terms, when each partner in a relationship develops a synthesis of male and female energies inside, with the streams running the right way, then they will open to the possibility of being guided by the universal flow of the primal receptive and penetrative archetypal energies.

In this case, as poet Bill Holm told us,

If they dance together,
something unexpected will happen.
If they don't, the next world
will be a lot like this one.[4]

Gender, Spirit and the Sexual Soul

By now it should be clear that we see the differences between
men and women as also being a spiritual issue. If we are right,
then the conscious pursuit of relationship is also a spiritual
task, albeit not an easy one. How is this spiritual side of gender
borne out in human culture and history?

Many religions have at their core a sense of the interplay of
two opposing energies, often explicitly the masculine and the
feminine. The world is seen as having being created by this interplay, as well as sustained by their dynamic dancing at every
level. This was once thought to be a primitive anthropomorphic
fantasy – making gods out of people – projecting mummy and
daddy out into the sky. But the new advances in quantum
physics are beginning to guide us away from this view and
towards remarkable similar conclusions.

The exception to this metaphysical dance seems only to
appear in those religions based on the original Middle Eastern
myth that became the starting-point for orthodox Christianity,
Judaism and Islam, and these are the religions from which our
Western culture and thinking have sprung.

Ironically, the anthropomorphism is actually much more evident here; moreover, it is mixed with a political gender slant.
The generous, but sometimes punishing, head of the family,
Father God, creates a companion for lonely man from a spare
body part. When the ungrateful newcomer, woman, brings in
an awareness of difference – good and evil, naked and clothed –
he throws them both out of Eden. In other words, they are

punished for recognizing their genital difference. Through their guilty exploration of difference they are condemned to life of labour in exile from Paradise.

Essentially, the problems here are to do with gender and sex, and in consequence the spiritual hierarchies of these three religions were exclusively male. Women, the body and in particular sex became problems which were generally too difficult to solve from the basis of this world-view. In the early modern period, contact with a New World which did not share this philosophy did not have the effect of broadening the view but rather served to make it dig in. Even nowadays, in our psyches we are still stuck with the problem of our gendered sexuality that has religious backing.

And yet, despite our philosophical heritage, our own experience and common sense can guide us here. Perhaps we could say that our souls have a gender. Certainly, if we follow our natural development through, we recognize that it is the soul which is sexual. It is the soul that is intimate with another. It is our souls which have a life beyond our cultural and philosophic limitations.

At the level of our hearts, human beings are the same. Feeling this sameness is amongst the highest order of experience that we can know. For it is the heart ultimately that knows, that surrenders to the other, that brings about profound connection.

And what place is there for our other major energetic pole, our genitals? In relationships between partners of the opposite gender these genitals are different and complementary: they seek out the other, they want to receive and to penetrate. Through our genital difference we have the extraordinary ability to achieve a fusion out of which a new soul is created.

It is a power not to be underestimated, neither in our genetic make-up nor in our creative imagination. It is the dance of life that creates and sustains us.

PART 4
New Life

CHAPTER 11

Conflict, Commitment and Power

Indeed indeed, I cannot tell,
Though I ponder on it well,
Which were easier to state,
All my love or all my hate.
Surely, surely, thou wilt trust me
When I say thou dost disgust me.
O, I hate thee with a hate
That would fain annihilate;
Yet sometimes against my will,
My dear friend, I love thee still.
It were a treason to our love,
And a sin to God above,
One iota to abate
Of a pure impartial hate.

Henry David Thoreau

We have taken a brief look at how gender difference creates tension in couples. Now we are ready to consider how relationships between men and women offer a sure but difficult path towards self-actualization and self-empowerment.

We have seen how our past experiences determine how we design our specific relationship styles and how we attempt to manage ourselves and control our partners. Behind these efforts lies the secret and unconscious longing for perfect parenting, and however unrealistic this hope may be, the prospect of giving it up is met with resistance and resentment. Bonding patterns, the Pushme-Pullyou and the drama triangle are all attempts to prevent having to give up our most primitive but powerful bonding styles.

However, letting go of these is a precondition for a healthier life and a better relationship. So, if we want to continue down the road leading away from self-betrayal and towards our potential, then there is no lasting escape from what has been stalking us all along. This is the encounter with *conflict*.

Conflict

Why should conflict take centre stage at this point? The steps within each couple's dance in the dark eventually become only too familiar – dull, exhausting, repetitive and predictable – and yet their familiarity provides a kind of comfort. As we saw in Chapter 7, our learned safe distance for intimacy is a blueprint not easily changed. It might not serve our needs for adult intimacy, but it maintains our sense of identity, and while the child in us is still running the show, survival, belonging and having a role are far more important.

As long as the inner parent remains the refuge for our vulnerable child part, the prospect of conflict with our partner will evoke familiar survival priorities. Bonding patterns in particular are fuelled by inner conflicts and involve escalation to places of *apparent* increased power. If we wish to go beyond the kind of intimacy offered by our habitual relationship stance, we have to review our patterns of dealing with conflict.

But meeting conflict constructively demands that we have some *genuine* power at our disposal. The challenge is to learn how to stop betraying ourselves in exchange for love.

This is no task for a child. Nor are the inner parents genuinely powerful, for they are motivated by a child's need for security. Their aim is to protect vulnerability and control the expression of deep feelings – either anger or grief, whichever is our personal black hole – while licensing bouts of emotion, mostly blaming and shaming. Meaningful engagement with conflict involves the ability to tolerate a variety of feelings and to have choice whether to express them directly, without causing harm. Such emotional literacy forms the foundation of mature adult power.

This is where our attitude to anger and grief comes in. Long-term relationships which work well are rooted in a balance of give and take, and of opening up to one another, of tolerating difference and setting boundaries. Learning to accept that we have a right to be angry and that vulnerability is not a weakness paves the way for a healthy sense of self-worth. Self-worth is a twin of self-love and it is these two which, under the cover of conflict, are stalking us now.

Commitment or Control?

No relationship can come through conflict without commitment. In this case, by 'commitment' we mean more than just staying in the relationship. We mean also the willingness to risk becoming real with your partner. This goes hand in hand with being willing to learn to become real with yourself. The commitment is therefore not primarily *to your partner*, but *to your own growth* and development, and thereby *to the relationship*.

This is why doing your duty is not enough – staying together *for* the children, bringing home the money, supplying emotional comfort or sex, even though these things matter and cannot be dropped. This level of commitment to *maintenance* is just not enough to get your relationship onto the launching pad in order to blast the two of you beyond the gravity of polarization (with its power and control games) and into the very different atmosphere of *potent intimacy*. For that, nothing will serve but learning to love yourself, developing the ability to take responsibility for your needs and feelings, and gaining a realistic sense of your own power.

This commitment also means learning to be intimate in a new way, for while we may say we want intimacy, what we probably mean is that we want it as long as we can stay in control. In other words, we are willing to be intimate while it does not involve having to be vulnerable. Guarding vulnerability, however, is the antithesis of genuine connection with another human being. So we make some deal or other where we stay in control but ultimately betray ourselves.

It can be hard to see that there is any other choice, since we usually inhabit an emotional system in which only polarized options exist. This is not simply in our inner worlds, for our society's social and political structures often also seem to be based on such misleading and immature premises. The commitment we are talking about is to move beyond such oppositional thinking. It means developing the ability to bear the tension of difference and difficulty, even when the new way has not yet appeared.

Is it any wonder that it takes effort and time to begin to get a glimpse of the value of this? Like all soul work, it cannot be hurried, but it can easily be missed.

Learning to take responsibility for recognizing and being clear about our needs is like learning to become a new person. It demands that we accept that the responsibility for our welfare no longer rests with anyone else but ourselves. As long as we continue to protest about 'the impossible other' we stay focused on the past rather than the present: we *give* to our partner/parent the authority to make us happy or unhappy. In this way, rather than giving up any control, we *abdicate responsibility* for our own well-being.

Intimacy is centred around vulnerability. It involves taking risks and giving ourselves permission to have all of our feelings, needs and wants, even if our partners cannot meet them. Fundamentally, it means *giving up* control and in doing that we develop a side of ourselves which is very strong. Once we begin to give up the hope for perfect parenting and stop abdicating responsibility for our happiness, once we risk not maintaining control and once we choose to commit to our own growth and that of the relationship, we receive an unexpected bonus: *power*!

Power

Power is a difficult word. It has acquired the meaning of being in control over external circumstances or other people. Our culture is suffused with images of power – hundreds of films show raw power in action. Most of these are loveless, emotionless, ruthless and violent. We have all seen abuses of power and therefore power brings up some tricky associations for most of us. Consider the following for a minute:

What does power mean to you?
What do you associate with power?
What is your relationship to power?
How comfortable are you with your own power?
Do you recognize your own power?
What stops you from knowing and showing your own power?
What is your experience of other people's power?
Have you ever considered what power has to do with intimacy?

Perhaps you say to yourself: 'I don't want conflict in my intimate relationships — there's enough of it out in the world. What's wrong with me trying to avoid it at home, which is where I go to for peace and restoration? What's wrong with peace?'

But we believe that if you want to love, you have to develop a mature relationship with power. And conflict is a forum for power. We are also convinced that the misuse of power is usually driven by fear, and that learning to know and express your own power is an act of peace. If you are unable to trust your ability to protect yourself when needed, you tend to live in an emotional red-alert mode, with your actions and choices automatically prompted by fear. Since love and fear cannot easily co-exist, the result is the vicious circle of escalating emotional turmoil that we have described.

By continuing to allow our partner's behaviour to determine how we express our values and aspirations, we stay locked in fear-based collusion. The repression of undeveloped aspects of the psyche requires more and more energy to maintain a veneer of power. Whether this veneer is achieved by escalating into the position of a tyrannical parent, a self-denying smotherer or a helpless child, we stay stuck and discontent. We merely re-fashion the problem in different disguises until we permanently establish an unfulfilling marriage or yet another divorce.

Life will never be free of conflict. But we can choose to invest our emotional resources more beneficially. The first steps towards peace are the same in relationships as they are in politics. First a realistic assessment of our own power is required. Next, we can begin examining our fear of the other, challenging our rigid beliefs about their motivations. In any process of breaking down walls and building bridges it takes time to determine whether the new structures on either side will eventually bend and grow to meet each other across the abyss or will become two separate new walls. To build a strong bridge, the art is in learning to compromise without sacrifice. To create a sustainable potent peace both partners need to maintain a realistic sense of personal power.

Love and Personal Power

Power has many faces and uses. Like fire, it can destroy or be used for transformation. It cannot, however, be ignored or denied, especially in a relationship, where conflict is inevitable. Like any other aspect of life it is best to get to know its different forms.

Despite the changes in Western society in the area of what could be called 'role power' (professional, parental, economic, cultural, racial or gender), deep-seated attitudes to power still prevail. Men and women do not have the same experiences of power, through being raised with different expectations. A man is still seen as powerful when he exercises power over others, in what we could call 'coercive power'. In the positive sense, this is taking responsibility and showing leadership. A woman is more likely to be expected to exercise the kind of power which attracts, by means of her outward appearance and/or the relational style she adopts. Such power is associated with a promise of care and love, and has been called 'affiliative power'.[1] Both coercive and affiliative power have positive aspects, but the former easily turns into abuse and domination at the hands of an insecure individual. The latter, in its negative aspect, can also abuse, but more usually becomes the power of the victim in the martyr role. Both power styles have to do with self-worth and the tension between belonging and autonomy which we outlined earlier.

Whatever is unconscious in a person tends to end up controlling their behaviour. We are driven by whatever we do not consciously acknowledge. While the pressure of unrecognized feelings and needs builds up within, on the outside we may present an entirely different picture. Those who deny their power, or whose outer power style appears to be affiliative, are often driven by their disowned power needs such as ambition or self-assertion. Similarly, a person who is consciously identified with power is likely to be unconsciously driven by love needs, such as affirmation, belonging and acceptance. This is why, exacerbated by gender programming, men classically tend to have difficulties with expressing grief, while women can find it more difficult to express anger. Nevertheless, we should point out that there is a big difference between grief and self-pity – and some men can excel at the latter! Nor does having a hysterical temper tantrum or sulking really count as expressing empowered female anger!

We all long to take ownership of our innate potential, to experience ourselves as both loving and powerful human beings. By being constantly challenged and exposed in our intimate relationships, we are forced to question our reactions and behaviour, and to engage with our undeveloped sides. This pressure urges us to give birth to a different kind of power: *personal power*. Personal power, which arises from self-mastery rather than self-betrayal, stands in stark contrast to wielding internal control.

The signs of having achieved a degree of personal power are daring to develop some facility with the following:

- *We are able to tolerate our own feelings*. But we are not obsessed with them. This is particularly important with grief and anger, the latter being the feeling most associated with the energy of power.
- *We are able to receive the feelings of the other*. Less driven by our own feelings, we can tolerate our partner's.
- *We are able to know our needs and ask for what we want*. We may not always get what we want, but we are not afraid to stand alone and express it.

- *We are able to say 'no'* and stand by it.
- *We are able to protect ourselves* without being busy manipulating the other.

In other words, we become 'I'-focused rather than 'you'-focused. The paradox is that by empowering ourselves we become more willing to be vulnerable and open to the other.

It was a Friday night and the café-restaurant was alive – busy, full and noisy. They were sitting at a table near the door with their friends Simon and Louise. They had been there for 20 minutes and no one had ordered yet. The waiter had moved off for the third time, with a show of long-suffering patience.

Louise was preoccupied with her diet and what she could not allow herself to have and the other three had not wanted to override her.

'Perhaps I should just have the salad on its own?' she suggested languidly.

Simon was being pretty cool, perhaps a trifle over-chilled, but eventually he could stand it no longer. 'If you don't want potatoes you don't have to have any – it's up to you,' he said with veiled exasperation.

'And then can I have some of your chips?' she appealed, looking up at him with her best little-girl face and a flutter of eyelashes.

But Simon would have none of it. 'No way,' he answered, 'make your own choice. You can have chips yourself – you don't have to eat them all!'

Simon was beginning to sound punishing and Louise looked even younger.

On the other side of the table she was beginning to feel uncomfortable. It was none of her business, but she decided to risk it anyway, and stepped in to rescue her friend: 'Oh come on Simon, you'd give me a chip if I asked, wouldn't you?'

'Of course I would, darling,' he replied flirtatiously, and to cover being wrong-footed he changed direction. 'What are you having?' he asked his friend who was staring at the menu like a man in a dream, pretending not to be aware of the atmosphere at the table.

'Oh, I dunno, what are you having, love?' he passed the buck on to his partner.

There was a slight pause.

'I'll have the steak,' she announced with a strange sense of triumph. 'That's what I want.'

'You're having beef?' said Simon and Louise together, as if they had rehearsed it, their eyebrows extended heavenward.

But nothing could touch her, she felt solid and warm inside.

'Yes,' she said, 'that's what I want.'

Power, Anger and Wanting

Our relationship with anger is often an obstacle on our path to developing personal power. Whereas we might be quite willing to accept our own anger as our means to stand our ground, when it comes to our partner's anger it is a different matter. We may be afraid of being on the receiving end of strong emotions or our partner's anger may actually be *aggression*, which we quite rightly reject.

Aggressive or defensive anger is the weapon of someone who fears loss of control. It tends to come out of nowhere and to be out of proportion to the event that triggered it. It is accompanied by blame and accusations, and tends to escalate into slamming doors, smashing plates or even physical violence. Alternatively, it may take the form of icy sarcasm, a punishing stone wall or the tendency to humiliate the partner in public. Whichever way, it leaves the recipient feeling powerless, raging or in despair.

This kind of anger is not the healing force that we are talking about, but the reaction of a person who doesn't trust that an assertion of their will can have any effect. The real enemy, of course, is within. A person addicted to aggressive anger is liable to favour a coercive power style and a persecutory relationship mode. Unchecked, the effect of this is disastrous, because it ensures that the partner never feels safe enough to be vulnerable and is forced to reply in kind.

It is possible, though, that your partner actually *is* expressing clean anger to assert their rights, but that you are unused to this or have bad experiences with angry people in the past. You, therefore, *experience* it as aggression. It frightens you and makes you feel very uncomfortable, even hated. This probably means that you are not at ease with your own anger. You may be someone who never gets angry; whenever you get upset, you cry or go quiet, waiting for the trouble to pass. Whatever the reason, you can't see any excuse to justify anger.

You probably also feel taken for granted, used, never really listened to. It is unlikely that your sex life is ideal. But it's not easy to admit, because that would be saying something about what you want, and internally you are not allowed to do that. You may have ways of getting what you want, but you never ask it directly.

Now, the force behind clean anger is the same force which is behind wanting and the ability to articulate what is important in your life. If you can't access your anger, you can't assert yourself, and you will be unable to say what you want or to put down firm boundaries around yourself. If you can't express a firm 'no' then you can't say 'yes' wholeheartedly either. How then can you possibly let your partner know who you really are?

Under the surface, in your unconscious, your anger will keep on growing, for unconscious anger is bound to control you. Eventually it will have to come out. Anger, therefore, needs to be put in context and befriended.

There are three stages to the emotion of anger. First, you must be able to recognize and feel it as it arises. Many people have denied it so strongly that this can be a problem in itself. Secondly, you must be able to express it without being taken over by it. It also needs to be received by someone or you may end up feeling impotent. Lastly, it needs to be expelled without causing harm – you can roar and swear, thump a pillow or beat the ground.[2]

The classic man of action went straight from feeling anger to expelling it – and usually someone got hurt. He bypassed expressing it, which is the crucial part, so never learned to be clean with it.

Although discomfort with anger used to be a classically female stance, these days we increasingly hear from men in such a predicament. When we explore this further, it often turns out that they are afraid that their anger will kill if they let it out. Our usual response is to confirm this possibility. Then we ask what price they are paying for negating their powerful feelings. Invariably, the cost turns out to be their zest for life, their pride, their passion. To protect their loved ones they sit on their anger, and often the loved one appreciates it. But they also say to us:

> If only he wasn't always so tired or depressed. If he would only be more outgoing ... I know I shouldn't say it ... a bit more 'manly'.

By this, the woman does not mean that she wants a barbarian in the house, because these men are right – unrestrained rage can kill. But the truth is that women do not feel safe around men who are frightened of their own power.

Experimenting with Raw Power

Familiarity with the three phases of anger involves skills which can be practised and learned. In some of our workshops we give people an opportunity to experiment. We provide a safe environment, a rule of no physical contact and enough people around to stop anyone who might lose control. We then invite people to express non-verbally all the anger they never expressed, while being face to face with their partner. Very interesting things happen.

Sometimes a man, confident of protection from the damaging potential of his power, eventually allows himself to experience his anger in its full strength in his body and then to express and expel it. It is often accompanied by loud roaring, flushed skin and trembling. With shining eyes he looks straight into the eyes of his woman. It may be the first time she has ever seen him like this.

Sometimes the woman shrieks and wants to runs away and hide in tears. Despite the safety of the exercise, she is in obvious fear and distress. When she has calmed down, she often has a story to tell about being at the receiving end of the destructive expression of anger from a father or a brother, when her own angry impulses were drowned in fear. And, to no one's surprise, the man has a matching tale about seeing or experiencing male misuse of power. He perhaps made an unconscious promise to his mother that he would never become such a man. Both learned to repress and disown their own anger, and invariably it turns out that their relationship lacks juice.

Another woman may react by giggling; she finds it hard to maintain eye-contact. If her partner is put off by this, which he often is, they both become shy and start playing around like kittens, nervous laughter releasing the tension. Afterwards they tend to feel let down, sad, irritated. They have both been reminded of a lifelong double bind: if they feel their anger, they may be tempted to express themselves as strong and powerful and then they feel guilty. And if they give into that guilt, they feel shame about being too weak. The guilt is related to the wish to separate from the internal parents, to be autonomous. Years ago, this wish was somehow experienced as threatening to one or both parents, maybe a single parent who scarified their own happiness to bring up their child and wasn't able to fully hide their envy at the child's advantage. Alternatively, the child was used as a buffer to cover the emptiness between the parents and any move towards independence was greeted with an air of panic. The shame which the couple now feel is about how they continue to betray themselves in the present.

In another scenario, the man is not put off by his partner's shyness. Suddenly, something is fired in the woman and she joins in with the growling and shouting, the flushing and trembling. Afterwards, they can't take their eyes off each other. They like what they see with their shiny eyes. They like what they feel in their bodies. They wish the group would leave the room so they can finish what they've only just started.

Of course, similar scenes can also occur with the gender roles reversed. It is amazing how much information about our own and our partner's relationship with power can be obtained from a simple exercise, and how much a couple can learn about their sex life from such an experience!

Without the ballast that comes from knowing we have power at our disposal, we cannot trust ourselves enough to dare to open up to our partner. Willing abandon is therefore not possible. Constantly being on guard against disapproval, rejection, judgement or abandonment, whether from within or without, does not open the door to intimate sharing or free sexuality. If, however, both partners learn to be at ease with their power, with their feelings, they can have a relationship which includes vulnerability and passion.

Love and Inner Authority

We hope it will be clear by now why we believe it can be a sign of health and growth when a relationship hits conflict, *as long as the couple participates with the process*. But you need to have *commitment* and to develop sufficient *personal power* to reap the benefit. Otherwise you stay afraid of conflict, or addicted to it – both boil down to the same thing in the end. You have to join battle, as it were, *with* but not really *against* one another. Writer Sam Keen takes this idea up:

> Sometimes what looks like a fight is only the fierceness of love. At the moment, the honest struggle going on between a man and a woman is less comfortable but more loving than the old false peace. They have moved from a condition of silent hostility, buried resentment, and covert low-intensity warfare to open conflict. So, the first thing they need to do is acknowledge the strong, strange interchange that is taking place between them. They are wrestling together, changing roles in the hay, engaging in honest intercourse, yessing and k(no)wing each other. And contact is the first condition of love.[3]

When conflict can be faced and entered into, and the accompanying control games acknowledged, the eventual result is that there is actually less need for the use of force. Once the inner children have freed themselves from the need to control within, the energy previously used for survival is now available elsewhere – for spontaneous response, for example. And in the meantime, another process takes place. By repeatedly experiencing being at least tolerated for showing previously disowned parts of ourselves, a fuller sense of self is confirmed. Now, able to regulate our emotions in a much healthier way, we realize that our defended identity was not the true representation of our self, but a battle-fatigued survival personality.

This part of a couple's journey is a transformative shift from *surviving* to *living*. As we learn to trust our rights and take responsibility for our own needs and feelings, we gain a realistic sense of our power, and the fear of the other diminishes. No longer reliant on the other to affirm our rightness or acceptability, we can finally relinquish our parental projections. With a truer sense of ourselves, we begin to be able to have more compassion for ourselves, and thereby for our partner. We can see the other as both powerful and vulnerable, imperfect yet lovable.

Without personal power we cannot ever be truly compassionate. But once we know our own worth, fear of abandonment diminishes. Fear of rejection gives way to freedom of self-expression. Once we know we are powerful, we can choose how to apply our power. Being empowered from within paves the way to be willingly vulnerable and receptive. By committing to our own choices, asserting our will in relation to what we want and learning to express anger as clean communication, we are learning how to love.

What these changes amount to is a qualitative shift of authority. Once the need for rigid control of our feelings passes, once the urge to blame the other drops away, authority begins to move from being *internalized* to being *interior*. Guidance moves away from the inner parent, inner critic, inner perfectionist, to a new healthier *adult* centre. There is no longer a need to overvalue or devalue authority figures, since authority no longer rests on outgrown messages from the past. Genuine power is ultimately about having *inner authority*. Then we begin to hear a voice inside which recommends stepping out of the known survival mode. The Jungian analyst Mario Jacoby describes this shift:

The criterion (from the Greek *krites*, judge) resides finally within each of us. If we learn to listen closely, we can make out something like a 'voice' of the inner Self and develop a sensitivity for what 'sounds' right for us. This personal voice may not speak loudly and may become audible only after significant 'trial and error.'[4]

The 'trial and error' part is important. We never get it right in one go, but intimate relationships give plenty of opportunities to practise!

CHAPTER 12
Untangling the Web

Don't you care for my love? she said bitterly.

I handed her the mirror, and said:
Please address these questions to the proper person!
Please make all requests to head-quarters!
In all matters of emotional importance
please approach the supreme authority direct!
So I handed her the mirror.

D. H. Lawrence[1]

Fishermen, though they may be dreamers, are both brave and patient fellows. They risk their lives on the turbulent seas and wait for hours staring into water. When it comes to untangling their lines and nets, they patiently do the task, whatever the weather. They know that their patience will be rewarded.

Such qualities are useful when consciously pursuing an intimate relationship. There may come a time when the truth batters on our door and we can no longer deny it. It may be that the polarization has become too much, or that one partner has upped the ante by bringing in a third party, or simply that we are just too tired to go on doing the same old unrewarding thing. Then we realize that the mess of our relationship warrants clearing up and we had better start with ourselves. All along, our partners have been holding a mirror up to us and we finally accept that we need to look directly into it.

Looking into the mirror and untangling the web is not a once and for all task. Nor is it particularly easy: your self-image can get quite a bashing. But it is worth doing, because the reward is a more mature, more soulful image of yourself – and of your partner. It needs to be done day after day, regularly and constantly, as part of relationship hygiene. It's a psychological workout which gradually builds strong relationship muscles; after a while you can get to like it. It is a discipline which has to be committed to in order to reap rewards from your relationship, in the same way that fishermen commit to untangling and mending their lines and nets every morning, so that they reap their rewards from the sea.

The Mirror to One Another

So far we have been promoting our belief that there is a purpose to falling in and out of love. The process of losing ourselves in the other in order to find ourselves there later is one of profound complexity. We started out in a veritable hall of mirrors; now we realize that we are lined up in front of just the right mirror to show us who we really are. The difference at this stage of the journey is that now we see that *we* are not who *we* thought we were, rather than saying this about our partner. It is like coming out of the fog – a shift from focusing on disappointment to seeing with a sobering clarity.

When we were originally attracted to the other we were in a dream. It was a dream in which we needed the other to 'carry' certain aspects of ourselves that we were not yet ready to acknowledge or develop. Usually what attracted us to our partner was something that we could not be in our families of origin. Most partners make a miraculously precise fit: they compensate for their own lack by teaming up with someone who, in the beginning, seems to be the very embodiment of what they lack.

In our own story, we shared how a regimented part in Nick fell in love with a laid-back part in Helena. The fit between the apparently organized and serious (parent-like) partner and the apparently carefree or foolish (child-like) one is one we see quite a lot of in our counselling practice. This may be because the majority of our clients tend to be white middle-class Britons, where such a match seems quite common. A partner with low self-esteem teams up with another who is apparently self-confident and assured.[2] Or again, one who was kept childish in their family of origin finds a partner whose parents required them to be the grown-up. Together, they sense they can make it work; and they are right – but not until disappointment teaches them about the need to learn the art of untangling.

We cannot explain how we zoom in on each other so fast and with such accuracy. It must remain a mystery to do with minutia of observations our body-mind makes of the other. We assume that we are primed to recognize one who may be able to answer our most deeply stored and cherished longings. This phenomenon operates most clearly in what is called 'love at first sight'. Hazlitt, the early-nineteenth-century English writer, had a similar thought:

> I do not think that what is called Love at first sight is such an absurdity as it is sometimes imagined to be. The idol we fall down and worship is an image familiar to our minds. It has been present to our waking thoughts, it has haunted us in our dreams.[3]

There is a mysterious promise which we invest in our lovers: *they will be the one to make us psychologically whole.* We need another person to help us acknowledge those parts in us which we would rather not show and to develop what was arrested in us. But the promise is not just illusory, for it is related to something which is true in the partner. Both partners bring a unique gift from their family of origin: some aspects which the other could not be. Generally, there is a price to pay, for they also bring a curse: behaviour or attitudes which the other finds intolerable. But this is the mutuality of relationship – you don't get one without the other, because each needs the other to 'become whole'. The beloved does us a profound service by permitting us to use them as a screen to project onto. And we repay in kind.

The Mirror of Projection

'Projection' is the word psychologists use for putting unwanted parts of ourselves onto, or into, another person. We could say that each partner projects onto the other qualities which they are uncomfortable about admitting and aspects which they would like to develop. The first sign that we are ready to begin to recover or develop a particular disowned quality is when we find that part of the other irritating. Irritation often turns out to be a sign that we ourselves have business with that particular quality or attitude.

Projection is frequently considered to be a pathological symptom, but we prefer to see it as a developmental process. For the time being, we need the other to 'be it' for us, because we can't yet accept 'being it' ourselves. It is part of being an interdependent human being. When it comes to taking projections *back again* we radically transform our psychological worlds by widening our identities and our relational horizons. Psychology writer James Holis suggests that withdrawing projections:

...leads one to recognize that what one perceived was not actually real, that one was not experiencing the Other out there, but the Other in here ... The next stage requires the search for the origin of that projected energy within oneself.[4]

There are two movements here. The first is developing or acknowledging the qualities which we were previously unable to own. This can come as a bit of a shock. When the partner reveals, for example, that they did not in fact have the impeccable self-esteem which we projected onto them, we may initially feel upset and let down. Nevertheless, it was the projection that got us together in the first place!

With the second movement, we start to experience our partners anew, freed from the burden of our projections. We now have a chance to relate to them afresh, as beings whom we as yet hardly know. In other words, in taking responsibility for our own lives, we also reawaken a childlike curiosity about the other as a unique being. It can be a new beginning for love.

If we fail to do this, however, we may continue to use our partners for our own ends. Projection becomes pathological in relationships when partners consistently refuse to withdraw them. In such cases, people remain, as psychoanalyst Tom Main warns,

...not truly married to a person, but rather to unwanted, split off and projected parts of themselves.[5]

Shedding light on projections is the first function of the mirror. But there is another side — a fiery one. At the same time as carrying our projections, our partner spends a great deal of time with us and gets to know our less attractive parts very well. To be a good mirror for this side of our character — if we want to recognize our unconscious behaviour and grow into being the most complete person we can become — a certain amount of *non-acceptance* from our partner is required.

Such a statement may go against the grain. Many relationship pundits recommend unconditional acceptance. But we believe that our partners' refusal to tolerate all our compensated and survival-based behavioural strategies serves to reflect back to us the unhealthy sides of our adaptive personality. If we so choose, we can then learn to recognize the precise ways in which we settle for our 'safe distance for intimacy'. We are faced with those parts which, in the comfort of our old self-image, we would much rather not have recognized in the first place. We certainly do not enjoy having our worst sides hurled back at us. Yet only by entering this dream of love can someone get so involved with us to notice, feel and reject them – and then, perhaps, help us wake up. Here is psychotherapist Chris Robertson:

> It is no accident that the primary motive, the hidden agenda in any relationship, is a return to the source, the yearning for the beloved. So we bring ourselves to relationship with scant knowledge of ourselves, we seek identity in the mirror of the Other, who, alas, is seeking the same in us. With a thousand adaptive strategies derived from the fortuities of fated time, fated place, fated Others, we contaminate the frail present with the germs of the past.[6]

Chief amongst the uncomfortable sides of ourselves which we will want to recognize are the issues of:

- how like (or reactively unlike) our caretaker models we are
- how we tend to manipulate the other for our own ends
- how, fearing the unknown, we tend to replicate the familiar miseries of the past.

It is always uncomfortable to acknowledge such things in the mirror. We well may have to realize that we are utter beginners in this business of relationship, that we have little idea of what it means to be intimate, no matter how long we have been trying. Nevertheless, it is a crucial step for each partner, and for the relationship itself. In this way, a union can shift from one which is bonded in unconscious needs and behaviour to one of adult responsible partners, ready to commit to each other again. This re-commitment can now be made from an awakened reality and marks the start of a new phase – we call it 'learning to live the dream awake'.

When she finished speaking he began to breathe normally again.

He had been listening hard. It had been an effort. He had been forced to screw himself to the spot. She had been talking for a good quarter of an hour and he had said nothing, sitting with his head bowed. He had tried to stop his mind from wandering and managed it. He was pleased with himself. He tried to assess to what extent the many grievances she related were true, to what extent he was that creature she described.

Yes, he knew he was selfish, and often cowardly, and that many of his moves in their relationship disputes were defensive, like those of a frightened animal. He could see that often in an effort to protect himself he lashed out verbally, and could hurt her. He was sorry that this continued to be so, even when he was trying to train this out of himself. He wanted to stop being such a loner. He knew that he had learned lifelong ways of coping without getting his needs met, so that partly he no longer really expected them to be met. And that he had ways of making sure that he could get what he wanted without making himself overtly vulnerable. He knew that this made him extremely hard to live with and must infuriate her.

But why was she so focused on him? What was that about? Why did that not seem to change? Their couple counsellors had suggested that they each consider what might be the gift and the curse they brought to the relationship. Could it be that he was the only one in the relationship that brought difficult things? It could not be that he had the monopoly on curses – could it?

He caught himself feeling sorry for himself and quickly dismissed this thought. That was the old way. He knew he had done enough of that. At that moment he wanted to do things differently. He looked up at her.

He wanted to tell her that it was not the way, that she would stay stuck by being still so keen on describing his faults. But he did not know how he could say this to her in a way that she could hear or without becoming too pompous. He felt sure that she would think he was trying to put her down, when in fact he wanted to reach out to her. He wished he had more confidence in his relational skills at this moment.

The truth was he did not know how to reach her.

But he wanted to.

The Mirror Dance and the Infinity Pattern

Our untangling work presents us with the opportunity to re-evaluate how we manage the dilemmas which relationships evoke. Earlier we suggested that it was not easy to negotiate a balanced path through the dilemmas of power and vulnerability, dependence and independence, aloneness and togetherness. These dilemmas can be temporarily solved by recourse to the distancer-pursuer dance, which specializes in coping with excitement and control, and the bonding patterns, which demonstrate and externalize the parent/child conflict in the psyche. The mirror of self-reflection sheds much light on these patterns. But it involves considerable work to deconstruct what has become habitual. The main impetus to do this labour is the realization of how limiting such patterns can be.

One day, while examining the diagrams we drew in order to explore the bonding patterns which were undermining our own relationship, we noticed the way the energy was circulating. It went around in loops between inner child and inner parent, from top to bottom and back again.

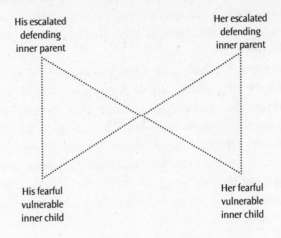

We saw that a particular shape was being traced, reminding us of a figure of eight on its side. In mathematics this is the symbol of infinity. We were chillingly reminded that you could stay in such patterns forever, going round and round in circles, never getting off, leaving your children to either finish the business for you – or repeat it endlessly themselves.

Despite the seriousness of being eternally locked into bonding patterns, they do have some value. They provide the prime means for evoking the material we need to bring to consciousness in order to grow up psychologically, and the pure physics involved can be taken advantage of. The dynamic energy inherent in a bonding pattern can be harnessed by the *will to change*.

In the energetic exchanges, a person's inner child starts to reach out (albeit confronting and blaming his partner/externalized parent) rather than recycling the energy internally (having to conform to the dictates of the inner parent). This is a first step towards freedom, towards taking generating power away from the internalized authorities. There is a trap in getting stuck in externalizing the energy, but this tends to present so much havoc that each partner – if they are prudent – will eventually receive an impetus to look deeper into what is going on. If not, they will move away dissatisfied, probably to repeat it elsewhere with another partner, for something in us seems to want to highlight these tendencies in order to refine them.

The secret behind the transformative use of energy lies in the very nature of the sexual charge created by the polarity between men and women. In this book we are focusing on the context for possible transformation within relationships, so there is little space to discuss the particular application of this energy here. The same is true for specific details of information arising from working with the bonding patterns, which allows individuals to resolve what we call their 'Oedipal riddles'. We will come back to these issues elsewhere. Meanwhile, we cannot move on without alluding to one remaining important obstacle.

There is a further element which complicates the ability to benefit from the energetic charge between partners. This is the tendency for human beings to replicate misery. The manifestation of this can sometimes defy all comprehension. Despite all attempts to reframe conflict as an opportunity, some couples stay locked in patterns which, though clearly dysfunctional, seem resistant to any attempt to break their grip. These may be in the form of a dynamic Catherine wheel of chaos or an endless immobility.

In each case, either one or both partners has a tendency to sabotage any attempts at change. If this comes from only one partner it may be that the other plays a more passive but collusive role. It is as if the relationship is exhibiting a strange addiction to unhappiness. In Chapter 6 we pointed to the tendency to reproduce the known misery of the past as a perverse security measure. The part responsible for such tactics in a person is known by psychotherapists as the 'internal saboteur'. It can have a field-day in a relationship. If both partners are prone to such activity, the relationship is liable to remain in deep trouble.

What is this addiction to suffering all about? It is a profound puzzle, probably a bizarre expression of loyalty to the inner child, who suffered so much and proved it was possible to bear life by sticking to the familiar ways to stay safe.[7] After all, if you learned as a child that no one was reliable enough to lean on for protection and consequently developed some survival tricks which worked, why abandon them as an adult? Having once learned to live without love, it may be too painful to open to the longing for it. Being at the receiving end of hatred or just simply being ignored is less threatening.

Compassion for the Task

Popular psychology sometimes runs the risk of creating a cult of the inner child while offering few ways of going beyond its internal tyranny. We think a committed relationship is the best chance for healing the inner child, but considerable inner work may be required to go beyond bonding patterns. Those who have a tendency towards the parent part will have to practise vulnerability. Those who tend to be the wounded or misunderstood ones will have to focus on their assertiveness or power.

For a partner to stop their instinctual tendency to respond from a critical inner parent in persecutor style, for example, is a huge task of deconstruction. It requires much will-power, self-awareness and determination, as well as remorse for hurting their partner. Once the couple can talk about these hurts more explicitly, things will improve – but they also have a tendency to get worse before they get better.

There is an order to the healing process. First comes non-acceptance of the habitual pattern in the other and in oneself; then comes the dedication to the long hard work of untangling all the threads. However, the baseline is that compassion for oneself and for the other is the only sure method of transforming bonding patterns and freeing the inner child.

Knowing that one's partner is fully committed to the relationship creates a secure-enough container to face what is revealed in the mirror dance and to endure what the other projects. Equally, only commitment provides the time-scale needed to reach beyond survival. An attitude of 'I'll stay as long as it feels OK', whether verbalized or not, inevitably prevents the partners from dropping their defences. It is precisely through testing the other's willingness to tolerate both our worst and best parts, and our own increasing self-recognition and self-acceptance, that over time we relinquish the need to be in control.

With this loosening, our feelings flow more spontaneously. Sometimes, the untangling may at first result in a deep sense of grief, melancholy, longing, or a strange restlessness. If a couple can learn to honour, share and not fear these feelings – even when there is no obvious reason why they surface – a far-reaching healing can take place. But if they are not recognized as a release of energy – like water gushing from ice melting in the warmth of a spring sun – we can mistake what is happening. A breakthrough can feel similar to a breakdown in the initial stages. A well-meaning partner can panic: 'Oh no, what have I done – or not done – now? I can't believe we are back here again!'

It takes a lot of awareness and personal power to not fall back into bonding patterns and drama triangles at this point. In fact everyone does, it's inevitable. Don't despair. Your relationship is initiating you into a new order of things. It's bound to be difficult. Once you are aware of being stuck again, flag it up, allow some time to let things cool down and forgive yourselves. Then once more summon up the courage and trust to open the doors to love. This is a very tender and delicate process. When allowed, the grief will meet a quiet yet powerful joy. When grief and joy can live in the same house, compassion for the task which both partners have to undertake becomes possible.

Using the Mirror Wisely

As you become skilled in using the mirror of self-reflection you also become more able to see what is going on for others in their relationships, including your partner. But here comes a health warning. Anything you come to know about the other only helps if it releases compassion through understanding. Otherwise, however clever you are about the other, you remain stuck with them as the problem. You then use your partner to rationalize your unhappiness. You start fresh bonding patterns and Pushme-Pullyous. It is very easy to leave the high road of self-responsibility and get back to the safe distance for intimacy. Every exit leads directly back there.

Only what you discover about yourself can help you make choices about your own behaviour. It is not difficult to be critical of your partner and easier still to criticize when the going gets rough. On the one hand it helps the partner, because you, who know what it's like to be at close quarters with them, offer up the mirror. But the mirror is for looking into, not for wielding as a weapon. That's why the best analysis in the world is not guaranteed to help, unless it's about yourself rather than the other. It isn't so difficult to see the stuck places in others' relationships. It would be easy to counsel couples if all there were to it were spotting faults. But the skill lies in enabling others to take on your insights as their own and to use them for change. It is most unlikely that you will be able to be neutral enough to do that for your own partner. Well, we find it difficult!

Spotting bonding patterns is an admirable skill to develop, of course; it is a tremendous relief when such things are named. The load is further lightened if humour can come in. But it must be genuine humour – not sarcasm, or at the expense of your partner, but sincere humour about the folly of life.

Another useful skill is to become a ruthless 'hunter to ourselves', relentlessly on the case of your internal saboteur. 'Well, I only wanted to keep you safe,' says he. To override him you have to find a voice which is in command-mode: 'I'm in charge now,' you reply. Learning to accept the other and letting them be their own hunter – it's not your business in the end – is yet another skill worth practising.

Importantly, if you sincerely wish to get out of the clutches of bonding patterns and come to grips with untangling your web you will need to find a new gear – one which is not habitual. To begin with it will feel like hard work with little room for spontaneity. It's not unlike stopping smoking. No amount of external pressure or reason can make you quit the habit for good. Only your own decision will have any lasting effect. Even then, your choice will need to be reaffirmed on a daily basis for some time. To say 'no' to your familiar behaviour and your natural reactions, you will need to repeatedly remind yourself that you are freely choosing to say 'yes' to something new and not merely depriving yourself.

If you persist you will eventually experience a shift within yourself. A voice of inner authority, which we described in the last chapter, will come to your assistance. It is the voice of your adult self, which wants you to be your best. It is a voice which wishes you well.

Paradoxically, learning to develop this kind of inner authority is a prerequisite for compassion.

CHAPTER 13
Compassion

When men and women come together,
how much they have to abandon! Wrens
make their nest of fancy threads
and string ends, animals

abandon all their money each year.
What is it that men and women leave?
Harder than wrens' doing, they have
to abandon their longing for the perfect.

The inner nest not made by instinct
will never be quite round,
and each has to enter the nest
made by the other imperfect bird.

Robert Bly[1]

When we have accepted the need to untangle our fishing lines
and courageously looked into the mirror of self-reflection
which our partners hold up for us, it is time to look with different eyes at the creature we fished up. As we substitute fear
and safety-seeking with courage and compassion, we begin to

understand the complexities of who we have become and who the other may be. We recognize that it is a benign miracle that two people of different genders dare to live together. Relationship turned out to be more than we bargained for. Both of us deserve compassion for having taken the task on.

Compassion for the task of relationship involves being passionate about yourself. This is not a soft option – in fact there is a certain fierceness about it. It implies that you are rigorous with yourself. You develop a refusal to collude with the 'you' who willingly settles for familiar misery. You listen hard to try to follow the voice inside that can command you to do your best, rather than the one that invariably recommends safety. But being passionate about yourself does not mean being convinced that you are always right.

Having 'com-passion' for the one you're with means that you become good at putting yourself in their shoes, at understanding reality as it impacts them – not as you think it *ought* to impact them. You give them the 'benefit of the doubt'. Abandoning the longing for their perfection, you commit to them – fully. You still want them to be and do their best; you expect the same standards of yourself. But you now know in your heart and body what is important, and how difficult it is, and how delicate and scared people can be. It is worth remembering how fragile we all are, as singer Sting once poignantly reminded us.

Essentially, it means that you have compassion for each other and express this as a passion for what you are creating together, as the product of your love and as the transformation of your original unconscious attraction into a conscious and grounded reality.

What does this look like? Does it mean that you never argue or that you always agree? No, of course not. You may still not like your partner's weird habits, you may not always feel loving towards them, or want to spend all your time together. But it does mean that you stop allowing them to get under your skin and firing all your alarm chemicals, because you know that your relationship – that means you *and* the other – is the product of your choice, your love and your creativity. And it can feel transformed – partly because there is more genuine peace. You are no longer so occupied with each other. From the outside it may not look very exciting or different, yet on the inside it can feel totally different. There will be something about you which people notice – a particular kind of attractive fragrance, something which gives a flavour of the bouquet that a compassionate relationship can give out.

One day, she awoke alone in the bed, still tired from the night before, when they had suffered yet another of those awful scenes.

But this morning something inside her was different. She had had enough. And this time she was not tempted by fantasies of leaving him and going off in search of her true destiny somewhere else.

No. She'd had enough of this stupid game they were playing with each other. She felt as though she had finally learned the lesson. After all these years, they were still together. They could even still be bothered to get upset by what the other did or didn't do. She knew, deep in her heart, that she loved him. Where she had been mistaken was that because she didn't always like him – as a matter of fact she frequently neither liked nor understood him – she had thought that they couldn't be right for each other, that it couldn't be love.

But she loved children, friends, cats – even herself – without any of them being perfect, so why expect it of him? She didn't want to put that condition on him. Right now, whatever his position was, she was going to do her best to change things.

'Morning!' she greeted the pale, stern face looking into an empty cup of coffee. 'You look as if you got as little sleep as me last night. I don't know what it is that happens between us, but even if you don't believe it right now, I love you and I want to find a way to deal with our difficulties that doesn't destroy us.'

'You love me! Great!' he countered in his best helpless ironic voice. 'Whatever do you want now? Look, I'm exhausted. I've got a meeting this morning and look at me! Please, just leave me alone, I've had it.'

As she felt him feeling sorry for himself she winced. She only just managed to fight off her habitual reaction to being rejected. But she didn't let herself start crying or yelling at him.

'I know what you mean. But I do love you, and I believe you love me too,' she said instead. 'It's just not good enough the way we are with each other. We both deserve better. Do you want some more coffee?'

'OK,' said he to the cup.

Moments later, on his way to the bathroom to shave, he couldn't help noticing that he dreaded the day less than when he had woken up. Occasionally he caught glimpses of her in the mirror, as she prepared herself for her day. She really did seem different, more in herself.

He wasn't sure if he trusted it. But he liked it. It scared him a bit, but he did notice how attractive she seemed, and even if he could never admit it to her, he rather admired her for her passionate outbursts. If only she would apply more of this energy to other things, life might be different.

As he drove to work he was still daydreaming about that difference. His eyes became moist. It was not unpleasant. But he had to acknowledge a slight uneasiness. He began to question himself. Could he really handle it if she still loved him after all they had been through? Could he trust it? He certainly yearned to be loved – he could admit that – but if it came knocking on his door could he really let it in? Sometimes even he wondered what that would be like to really know he was loved. He knew that he was sulky and sorry for himself in a way that he would never want his best friend Simon to see and that actually he ought to kick the habit.

So he decided to make a positive move towards her and tell that he knew he had a problem, that it wasn't all her. What should he *do? Phone her at her work as soon as he arrived? Ask her out to dinner or send flowers? Wasn't that all too corny? What if she rejected him again?*

'Ah, to hell with it! For God's sake, just do it, man!' said an unusual voice, out loud in the car.

Where on earth did that come from?

Grief as the Midwife for New Life

Compassion is not possible without free access to our hearts; it is not the same as feeling sorry for someone. While it is important that we have the emotional literacy to develop personal power, enabling us to fully say 'yes' and 'no', true compassion only comes about when we are voluntarily able to be vulnerable. In this context, the feeling which is most important is grief.

We may have given the impression that the disappointment and conflict in relationships lead *only* to self-awareness. In fact, self-awareness is useless if we cannot shed a tear or open our hearts. As a great sage once said:

> You may learn to levitate, but if you can't love you are but a flying idiot.

It is by helping us unpack our grief that self-awareness gradually lifts the veil so we can embrace a deep love, one which can hold our wounds and release our remorse.

A relationship will involve both wounds and remorse. Suffering is a major component between lovers. There are times in a relationship when the sense of being let down is a tragedy in which a person feels alone, trapped and deceived. Affairs and 'acting out' outside the relationship arouse feelings of betrayal which can last a lifetime. Sometimes unintended slights from the very first moments of relationship cause wounds which seem never to heal. There are many occasions in the course of love when one or other partner gets hurt. Such hurt is not imagined, it is real. Even when it comes about because one partner feels misunderstood and might feel differently if the full picture were revealed, hurt can do lasting damage.

Suffering is a major component between lovers. It is a quality intimately connected with the human soul and engaging with it enlarges the capacity of the soul. It can be avoided, but only by putting on a brave face, sweeping things under the carpet or cutting and running. But grieving for the misunderstandings, suffering and hurts caused in the relationship is vital. It is the same process as mourning for the dead – only when it's done are you free to get on with life, to move on to the next stage.

Such grieving needs to be done jointly. It is no good for one partner to be constantly grieving while the other impatiently waits for them to stop being so emotional. This simply makes the loneliness which both feel more pronounced. No, the grieving must be done together. Clarissa Pinkola Estes recommends making a map of the relationship and marking in the 'little deaths', like the shrines to road accidents that you see in Catholic countries.[2] All the hurts, wrong turnings, roads not taken, insults and grievances which happened in their sequence are to be plotted on a chart. We think it can be a good tool for healing, if approached with respect. But be aware, you risk stirring up things you might wish were better forgotten, feeling more misunderstood and getting into bonding patterns.

It is very easy to break the tension of grief by running back to patterns which escalate rather than staying with the pain. Most of us have worked hard in our childhood to come up with pain-avoiding relationship styles, so staying with it does require effort. But if you can share genuine remorse for betrayals and compassion for self-betrayals, even the worst of times can be converted. Grief is a natural quality of the soul – we do not have to *do* anything or learn it, only *permit* it.

Grief always deepens a person. It is universal; it cuts through all pretence. If we cannot permit grief in our lives, it will enter through other forms – perhaps depression, perhaps illness. Its avoidance will certainly create a void between partners.

Staying with the pain eventually softens and strengthens the heart. It enables us to love. Love means giving of our heart, and it takes an open and strong heart to tolerate grief and to share heart-felt feelings with another. When the grief can be embraced, a message is sent to the inner child that can override the lessons of the past. This message is: *Vulnerability is allowed.* Then, perhaps for the first time, the child in each partner can feel safe enough to open and connect with the other. As Hal and Sidra Stone say:

> The vulnerable child is the gateway to the soul. If one's child is not available, soul contact is very difficult with another human being.[3]

The Third Being – the soul of the relationship – can now make its presence felt.

Learning to Love

Vulnerability is certainly the gateway to the soul – but it is not the child who *opens* the gate to the other, or to the soul. The preparations are done by an alert, empowered and compassionate adult. It is the adult – our biological goal – who can master its own reality, for the sake of personal completion and voluntary intimacy. Then the opening happens naturally, by grace. It can take time for this and the soul's timing does not respond to any agenda. It may be a long time before we can say that we know something about loving.

Meanwhile, with the softening and strengthening of the heart, we are now ready to take our inner work a step further.

No longer engaged in defensive strategy, we are ready to put the key question to the mirror of self-reflection. This is:

How do *I* have difficulties in loving?

Now it starts to become increasingly important to focus on how we love now, rather than how we were (or weren't) loved in the past. Somatic therapist Stanley Keleman believes that:

What often goes awry is when adults seek to be loved as they were loved as children. The central therapeutic question is: how do people have trouble loving, not how they were loved.[4]

Now we know that we have to learn how to love as beginners. If we apply our will, we can learn to inhibit the strategic habits of seeking love. This in turn will highlight how we avoid love, withhold love or manipulate for love. For many of us, quite specific messages will be mirrored back. Here Polly Young-Eisendrath describes some of the classic gender positions:

Paradoxically, confrontation with loss, resentment and frustration can open the door to the next stage of development for each person. For the man the next stage typically involves revaluing 'the feminine'. This process involves claiming his own dependency fears, needs and feelings, and expressing these openly. For the woman the process involves claiming her self-worth and authority of her own perspective, and integrating confidence into her self-image as a competent individual who has developed skills as a care giver.[5]

Finding answers to these questions can now be understood as a quest for personal excellence, the task of a compassionate warrior. The other is now a live feedback system, a barometer of intimacy, a companion on a similar journey, but above all, someone to love and not fear. The solution is not knowledge or self-mastery – these are only the means – but love.

We may never fully understand our beloved. But does it matter? With compassion, our stance can become less heroic, more contemplative. Neither of us will ever be perfect, but fate has thrown us together. What for? Can we dare to dream again?

With grief no longer avoided and compassion available, present and future become more important than the past. Our curiosity awakens at the mystery of the other and what we might create together. As Sri Rajneesh said:

> Relationship becomes a mystery to be lived, rather than a problem to be solved.

In love, curiosity is valued over understanding, over skill in communicating. 'Wonder and open discussion,' says Thomas Moore, 'are more moist.'[6] Finally we discover that we are able to live alongside someone who is different. If only nations would learn this too!

Learning to live with difference enriches our hearts and deepens our lives. Notions of perfection lose their meaning. Sometimes we still find our relationship too close, too stifling, and we need air. We need to stretch for some freedom; but once satisfied, we notice how the thing turns. Now we long to return home, to where we are rooted. It is as if now, close to the heart of the Third Being, we rest on its chest, feeling its lungs stretching and expanding, contracting and emptying, mirroring the rhythm of life.

CHAPTER 14
Death

> To love means to embrace, and at the same time to withstand, many
> many endings and many many beginnings, all in the same relationship.
>
> Clarissa Pinkola Estes[1]

As we write, in our country hideaway, it is autumn. In the village, the grapes have been picked and are already stewing in the fermenting tanks. In the garden, figs hang dark and sweet, walnut trees drop their heavy fruit; their yellowing leaves will soon follow. The ground is littered with apples and chestnuts ready to be harvested by both man and beast. Migrating birds, leaving as well as arriving, grace the sky with their formation dances, like pure energy in motion. The squirrels, forgetting their shyness, leap from tree to tree, up and down, collecting and burying as many walnuts and hazelnuts as they can. For them the sales are on, and there is no time to waste! In the vegetable garden, the summer's beans make way for the winter cabbages. Stacks of firewood slowly grow, as we take our daily exercise, cutting the broken branches and fallen trees released by the forest.

Wherever we look, in the midst of fruitfulness, change and decay, there is abundance. And through all of it runs the river, ever-changing with the seasons – watering the garden during the dry days and, equally important, draining the surplus in the wet season now to come. When the waters flow strong, the river's flexible identity permits the banks to simply overflow. In drier times, it runs more slowly and quietly, singing to itself and to those who know how to listen. As long as there is water the river runs, always in the same direction, assured in its own being.

Nature is a seasoned lover.

Savouring the natural beauty of this activity, we are touched by an overwhelming sense of rightness: everything in its own time, everything in its own place. And yet there is a seriousness here which, seduced by the apparent harmony, we could overlook. For winter is approaching. Life is about to become harder, food scarcer; the warmth of the sun is gradually diminishing and temperatures will soon plummet. The season of death is approaching.

But do the animals panic or despair as the preparations take place? They work hard, but if they believe that life is not fair, it is hard to tell. It's as if the beings of nature remember a secret we have forgotten, a secret about life and the laws of nature, about natural cycles: from life to death, from death to life. Every living organism will die sooner or later. It is the only absolute in life. Yet every time spring comes around again and we are amazed: it is as if we can hardly believe that the leaves have come back, that the flowers have bloomed once more. We see it again, for the first time.

Yet in our own lives, we tend to live with the idea of death as the enemy, so taboo, so dangerous that we hardly dare mention it. By not acknowledging its reality, we imagine we can fool it. In our intimate relationships we cannot fail but run into aspects of death and if we attempt to ignore them, we prevent a natural cycle of life from doing its work. Then the energy needed to sustain the health of our lives and promote joyful and passionate growth will simply not be available. We may vainly try to co-opt the methods of industrial agriculture and pump our lives full of whatever new products are on the market to avoid any wasteful fallow years, or try to plough another patch where the grass looks greener. But we will only impoverish our soil and prevent the natural ecology from composting and feeding in its own way.

Following the Call of Death

How does this metaphor help us think about the couple we have been following as they embark on yet another restless night or another day accompanied by heavy hearts and dark thoughts? Observing their struggle to find a mutually satisfying love, we might suppose that our couple's encounter with this idea of death is limited to 'flogging' the proverbial 'dead donkey'. Shouldn't we suggest they leave it for dead and accept that nothing can bring it back to life? They might not need too much persuasion.

We are at the edge of a great paradox. The irony is that until we reach the limits of our habitual ways of response, we will not willingly give them up. Such a surrender is not dissimilar to the experience of 'ego-death' as described in some spiritual disciplines. But – and this is the point – it is precisely through engaging with the struggle, looking in the mirrors, building muscle by running around in and out of bonding patterns and dying a thousand deaths that we reach a level of tension forceful enough to push through our known limits. The struggle for self-protection brings a relationship to the very doors of death. These doors, however, do not necessarily lead to the end of the relationship.

As far as we can see, relationships are always in development and have the capacity to move through specific levels. Each time the limits of a level are reached, something in the relationship wants to go forward and something else wants to hang on to the known. Our past experiences of endings will have a strong impact on how we meet each aspect of death within our relationship. There is pain and fear at leaving a particular level, for it is a death.

Earlier, we identified three major levels of relating: 1. maintenance, 2. polarization and 3. intimacy, or alchemy.

We see them in a sequence, but one which is not strictly linear, since it repeats itself at different times. The death in level one is falling out of love, or losing security or familiarity; level two is about moving through conflict or polarity into healing, which results from bringing understanding and compassion to the polarizations. To move into intimacy we leave everything familiar and strategic behind, and live in the unknown; it is a dangerous death and we resist it even when we think we want it. Access to each new level is guarded by death and we have to go through an initiation to reach the new life beyond.

If relationships are to do more than survive, successive deaths must be embraced, even though we have a natural inclination to resist them. Yet it makes no sense to continue to suffer or compromise if it doesn't lead to something else in the end. Without the understanding of a larger context, continuous conflict risks becoming futile defence or endless hostility – you can see the same thing in any report on world politics. What is challenged in lovers as they reach for a new level of relating is their habitual defensive way of expressing needs and feelings. Much of this will need to die. Ideas about the ideal lover – the longing for perfection – must also perish, as must, ultimately, all preconceptions about what love itself is.

If a couple can sustain the onslaught of attacks on their familiar ways of perceiving themselves and on their ideas about what a loving relationship should be, if they can feel that together they have the possibility of undergoing complete shifts in levels of functioning, then they may learn how to willingly enter this dying process and, in time, be transformed by it.

We know that the death of the old, if tolerated and borne, becomes compost for the new life already waiting to emerge. Until this is accepted, most efforts in a relationship can be seen as attempts to get the other to be different so that we ourselves can feel comfortable. Beginning to trust the wisdom of the life-death-life cycle of love presents us with the deeper challenge of learning how to respond to what is uncomfortable in ways that further our own awakening.

When people have no trust in this cycle, partnership too easily remains an exercise in handling the myriads of practical tasks that life present us with. Sex becomes the place to excite and frustrate our unrealistic expectations, and children risk becoming the battlefield of their parents' unfulfilled longings, aspirations and despair.

But respecting the process of dying in this way enables the relationship to create new life.

When Death Means the End of the Relationship

Not every relationship can survive and grow, for each one is unique and subject to its own fate. Sometimes honouring the life and wisdom of the relationship leads to a separation. Sometimes people hear a call and must follow it, whatever the consequences to their loved ones. It is as Thoreau says:

> If a man does not keep pace with his companions, perhaps it is because he hears a different drummer. Let him step to the music that he hears, however measured or far away.[2]

Throughout the life of a relationship, partners take turns at standing for one or other of two positions: one which maintains the boundaries of the relationship and one which serves to expand them. When these priorities collide, the couple are faced with difficult choices.

When we work with couples in deep crisis, we make it clear that we know relationships can feel very wrong, produce extreme states of pain and bring out shadow aspects of both partners that neither ever imagined. To us, these things may be signs that their relationship is inviting them to do important work. We respect the courage they show by bringing their struggles to the table, but we also know that everyone has a limit to how many deaths they can sustain. It is up to the couple to interpret whether the signs from their relationship indicate the need for a new birth or a final death. The heavy task of deciding when the end has been reached can only ever be taken by the partners involved. They alone have the mandate to declare their relationship dead.

The dilemma here is between responsibility to the destiny of one's soul and to that of the relationship. At such a moment people have to consider, as Sam Keen says, the serious question of 'Where am I going and who is coming with me?' and try to get the two priorities in the right order. This is never easy. But learning to be receptive to one's inner life, expressing genuine feelings and trusting in the life-death-life cycle of relationship must include having the courage to read the signs that signal the end.

Do both parties get the same messages? If one partner finds a relationship soul-less, it is unlikely that the other is genuinely fulfilled. It may be that the fear of being alone will make a person collude in mutual unhappiness, or keep hoping, against all odds, that one day things may change. Such passivity is unlikely to produce a good outcome. The change may manifest by a partner leaving and although it is understandable if the person left behind seeks to avoid the pain by blaming the departed, the question why they did nothing to prevent it will eventually have to be answered.

Without awareness of what you are responsible for, it is not possible, when a relationship ends, to harvest riches from your dance together. The only lasting way out of the guilt/blame-game is by assuming responsibility for your own life, informed by awareness of your own conduct, and thereby become the arbiter of your values. When *you* claim accountability over *your* life, no one can make you feel guilty or judge you, unless you let them.

If the two people involved can reach towards such awareness, their parting may indeed be an expression of the purpose of their relationship. The death of the relationship thus serves as midwife for new life. Here is Thomas Moore:

To sustain an ending – a soul death – without the defences of blame, explanation, or resolution allows the soul to achieve the new level of existence that only initiation offers. In outer life, that achievement may even look like defeat, but to the soul, death experiences like these are the only way towards true beginnings.[3]

It may take time to disentangle the threads woven round one another and it may need a healing ceremony in the same way that a marriage has one. Such attention helps a person to move on. Grieving cannot be avoided, but freedom may also be embraced.

Being Alone, Together

Whether we separate or stay together, the implicit issue is the ability to bear our own aloneness. Conflicts endured and sustained can act as a purifying fire in which the individuals refine their knowledge about their own deeper nature and values. The relationship, as it has been, will have to die.

Sometimes the experience of being loved can bring about the death of old co-dependent ways of being. Then a person can feel a new confidence in being lovable which can produce the energy to invest in their own life in a new way. They can start becoming 'selfish' in a way they never dreamed of and which may challenge their partner. But now, no longer so busy with the other, both have a chance at a new life together, one not based on making unconscious deals in exchange for belonging or a taste of 'That Lovin' Feelin' '.

Of course, it is important to be able to differentiate between indifference and detachment in terms of how the individual worlds are ordered within the relationship. Indifference signals the end of a soulful relationship, though a couple can still stay together for life, if they so choose. Detachment is the ability to recognize self and the other as separate while validating both – we are both in this relationship and the relationship is greater than the two of us. When detachment is first experienced it can be threatening, as it can feel similar to falling out of love. But when the inner sense of wholeness begins to be established, projection ceases and there is the possibility to really love and be intimate.

If that should happen to both parties, a great new love is born, one rooted in and sustained by Self-love – not self-obsession, but rather that each person is now in service of their own soul. No longer looking to the other to make them complete, each now assumes responsibility for themselves and chooses to honour their partner differently.

The poet Rainer Maria Rilke writes with extraordinary authority on matters of love. Perhaps it is because he spent the first seven years of his life raised as a girl by his mother and therefore, like the sage Teiresias in the myth of Oedipus, experienced both sides of the gender coin. Rilke suggests that the highest task lovers should set themselves is to be the *guardians of each other's solitude*. But he sees this as a mature achievement by those who have died to their preconceptions and learned from the cycle of life and death, from the starting-point of innocence, of 'beginner's mind':

There are such relationships which must be a very great, almost unbearable happiness, but they can only occur between very rich natures and between those who, each for himself, are richly ordered and composed; they can unite two wide, deep, individual worlds. Young people – it is obvious – cannot achieve such a relationship, but they can, if they understand their life properly, grow up slowly to such happiness and prepare themselves for it. They must not forget, that they are beginners, bunglers of life, apprentices in love – must *learn* love, and that (like *all* learning) wants peace, patience, and composure![4]

It takes a strong 'we' to be alone, together.

Meeting Death as an Ally

There is a principle in shamanism which suggests that death can be used as an 'ally', meaning a challenging agent for awareness and transformation. This is a powerful and fierce teaching. Such a death may be figurative, but it may also be literal. Rarely does a couple consider death as an ally in their longing for love. However, if one partner has to face a terminal illness or comes close to death in an accident, it may be that the shock brings a different perspective to what is important in their joint lives. If they can prevent the pain and fear of potential loss from increasing the distance between them, couples who come through such experiences together can emerge with a new lease of a very different life.

A woman in her late fifties once shared her moving story with us. An experienced and talented counsellor, she attended a short training in couple counselling which we were running. On the final evening, she told us that the most important thing she was taking with her was a determination to apply what she had learned to her *own* relationship. She had recognized how during more than 30 years with her husband they had fallen into a routine which betrayed the love and passion that once flowed between them. She knew she had played her part in letting that happen and she wanted to change it before it was too late.

We had the good fortune to work with the same woman less than two years later. In the meantime she had lost her husband to cancer. There had been no warning. He had been fit and healthy and looking forward to spending more time at their holiday home. Only months had passed from diagnosis to death. But these two wasted no time, and as she told the story the tears in her eyes were as much from joy and gratitude as grief. They had accomplished what they had set out to do.

She told us that on her return from the training weekend, for the first time ever she had spoken to her husband about her unhappiness in the marriage. She had also shared her longing for a deeper intimacy with the man with whom she had spent most of her life and had children by. His response had been defensive. He had felt accused and threatened. But she stood by her need for them to learn a different way of relating to each other. This led to them spending some time apart, to reflect separately on what they wanted from the rest of their lives.

On their reunion, something had changed in him. In her absence, he had missed her, *really missed her*. He had cried deeply for the first time in his life and this had opened his heart to his own longings. She had been right, he acknowledged, they *had* been in danger of missing each other. He wanted it to be different too. So they started to talk as never before. They went for walks and listened to each other's deepest thoughts and secrets. They were silent together, and the silence spoke. Love blossomed between them again.

And then he was diagnosed with cancer and given no hope of a cure. But it was too late for death to take their newfound intimacy away. Instead, they used death as an ally to make sure that not a single minute was wasted. With nothing left to defend against, they met each other. She ended her story:

It was as if all our years together had been leading us to this. We could so easily have missed it. The fact that we didn't made even the few months we had together like this worth everything that went before. I have no regrets. As a counsellor to other couples I have gained a lot. Now I speak from knowledge when I suggest that after death there is new life. The reason my husband and I could live through this eventual death as we did is because of the dying we went through before it.

CHAPTER 15

The Third Being

A man and a woman sit near each other, and they do not long
at this moment to be older, or younger, nor born
in any other nation, or time, or place.
They are content to be where they are, talking or not-talking.
Their breaths together feed someone whom we do not know.
The man sees the way his fingers move;
he sees her hands close around a book she hands to him.
They obey a third body that they share in common.
They have made a promise to love that body.
Age may come, parting may come, death will come.
A man and a woman sit near each other;
as they breathe they feed someone we do not know,
someone we know of, whom we have never seen.

Robert Bly[1]

In every intimate relationship there is a creature stalking the
partners. We call this creature the Third Being. This being has
a will of its own. It wants lovers to awaken and tends to wake
them up in rough and alarming ways, rather like a nightmare. It
wants each partner to find out exactly why they have dreamed
the other into their life.

Joining in this hunt with your partner and the Third Being is what we call 'pursuing a conscious relationship'. It becomes a kind of yoga practice which, in time, may lead to what some people call self-realization or a kind of 'enlightenment'. It is not a comfortable business, however, for being stalked by the Third Being and engaging in the process changes your life.

But this entity is also like a loving, embracing friend. A wonderful moment may come in a couple's life. Often it comes softly. It is unbidden, unexpected. At this moment the two realize that they are not alone: they feel the presence of a third. They realize that someone, or something, has been holding them, guiding them, right from the beginning. Through all the furious phases of relationship in which they did not know what was going on – falling in love, falling out, polarizing, distancing, pursuing, fighting, loving, looking in the mirror, trying to understand it all – they realize that they were guided all along. They have more than each other now, they have with them something beyond them both, a third presence: the Soul of the relationship itself. And despite its fierce teachings, this being is kindly; it has strength, wisdom and desire. It can hold a couple like a loving parent. But like all living beings it also has needs: it needs nourishment and protection. It must be stimulated and it needs time to develop trust, like a child. It is like a wonderful plant that thrives on water and regular attention; it must not be forgotten or allowed to get dry.

When a couple has a child a different and very tangible third being arrives. With the best of intentions, it is then easy to forget to nurture the relationship. In the busy, exhausting, unsupported life of nuclear families today there is little energy left for caring for yet another being, even when the children are in bed. But it is fatal to ignore the needs of the Third Being, for like an unwatered plant it may wither and eventually die. Or it may reappear as a lame, slumbering, unknown and frightening creature when the children leave.

Children and the Third Being

A man and a woman's biological destiny is fulfilled when they create a child. But in addition they need to develop a relationship in which the masculine and feminine energies are distinct and balanced for the child to get the best start and to get a taste for such a balance. They need some skill in managing conflict and in using the mirror of their relationship if they want their child to internalize the ability to live with difference and to learn how to love free from unnecessary strategies and compensations.

Achieving this harmony and alchemy is a great task and the couple need support. Ideally, support would be available from their parents, their community, friends, perhaps counsellors. Closer to home, it comes from being guided by the Third Being, who will push the partners to learn these skills. The problem is that the Third Being and the child, because they are both third beings created by the couple, are easily confused. A child comes from the *physical* aspect of a relationship, the Third Being from the *spirit* aspect. This is why couples who do not or cannot have children can be fulfilled by their conscious relationship itself, if they process any regret and grief they may feel at the lack of a physical child.[2]

The possibilities opened up by changes in society, like widespread reliable contraception and the new gender roles, give increasing choice whether to have children or not. Deciding not to have children is an option which speaks of a different imagination in the couple and needs to be respected. It will inevitably mean that in company they may have to justify their choice for saying 'no' to parenthood and this can be difficult, especially for the woman. Whereas a man's status goes unquestioned without the title of father, it is not yet widely appreciated that by such a choice a woman says 'yes' to a different archetype of womanhood. Furthermore, since children are no longer the inevitable consequence of sex between partners, the choice to raise a family now brings with it the responsibility of *consciously* choosing parenthood.

A couple who choose not to become parents can still create something which is greater than the sum of the two of them. They can give birth to what we call 'spirit children' – it may be a project, their work, a home or simply the energy between them. Besides, the deepest meeting is of hearts and the meeting of hearts creates something of the spirit on Earth.

Dyadic and Triadic Relating

In order to be fulfilled by their Third Being, and to bring up healthy children – whether physical or spirit children – a couple must do some 'homework' and be doing creative work, both together and alone. There is a danger that couples can use children as carriers of expectation, or to put something between the two of them, in order to have something to relate *through*. Then both the relationship and the children suffer. The quality of relating is corrupted and moves back to the immature state.

We call this kind of relating 'triadic' – there is always something between you and your partner. It's a three-way conversation. But when the Third Being is nurtured it takes over the space of the three, yet it holds you so that your relationship is one of 'dyadic' relating. You relate face to face, but are contained by the third – this is the best use of the inevitable triangle. Here David Miller comes at it from a similar angle:

> There is one man, one woman, and love. If this fails, then perhaps there will be one man, one woman, and a pet animal or a mutual hobby. Or there may come a time when she notes, not without appropriate jealousy, that he seems wed to his work, which is now a third in the marriage.[3]

There are many things that can fill the gap in such a triadic relationship. In sex it can be fantasy, or imposed standards of beauty or sexiness. Imagination is an important ingredient in sex, but when it turns into mental fantasy it impedes the curiosity about the other and becomes a third thing. The couple have something in between them and fail to find intimacy. Maybe an affair fills the vacuum which the two cannot face directly.[4] Often there is a tragic conclusion to such relationships. We think it best to invoke the benign spirit of the Third Being. The point is that the couple are two and whatever they create is the third.

The Third Being is not only a container and crucible for both partners, a reminder when things get grim again, but also a being with its own specific wisdom. It will teach you if you are willing to learn how to listen to it. Its messages are always very individual, for it speaks in the language of soul. However, by trying to listen to our own being, we have discovered that there seem to be certain general principles or laws which govern intimate relationships. We call them 'the sacred laws'. Although realistically the wisdom inherent in these principles cannot be passed on theoretically on paper, we will try to say something about the areas to which they relate in the next chapter.

CHAPTER 16
The Sacred Laws

The first retainer
he gave to her
was a golden
wedding ring.

The second – late at night
he woke up,
leaned over on an elbow
and kissed her.

The third and last –
He died with
And gave up loving
And lived with her.

Robert Creeley[1]

The sacred laws of relationship speak about the interplay of the two fundamental energetic powers, the creative receptive and the active penetrative, and by implication, a self-evident ethics which emerges. These powers have to do with the feminine and the masculine respectively in their archetypal or universal nature, but are not identical with the terms 'female' and 'male'. Their dance is to be observed from beyond a political perspective, where equality is already established and therefore taken for granted. This is an important point, otherwise it is easy to become reactive and fail to let the wisdom of the principles through to you. Because they come from the realm of spirit and soul, the laws are both precise and mysterious at the same time.

The laws speak of an inner alchemy in which we could say that a woman marries and is protected by an inner man, while a man courts and gives sovereignty to an inner woman. It may help you understand the subtle differences we are talking about if, while reading the following, you consider the kind of old-fashioned dancing in which a couple hold each other. When the man can provide an unfailing frame and mirroring of the woman, then she can do whatever she likes with abandon and surety. It honours their differences while giving both the experience of adding something beautiful to their joint dance.

• The primary principle is that the ground of all life is feminine. You may recall the XX chromosome, our common beginning, and you may also like to think of Mother Earth, our home. You know that all creative and created things come from a womb or an egg, both physically and metaphysically. By implication, ethically, the Earth ought to be honoured. She must not be over-exploited and deserves to be replenished. It means also that the feminine part of a person's psyche, the soul, is not to be ignored. The feminine principle, therefore, should command the ultimate respect, just as we can thank our mothers for giving us birth, even while struggling with our mother-complexes!

• It follows that whatever is born from the womb needs also to be honoured.[2] Whatever is young and powerless or vulnerable is to be cherished and protected. 'Women and children first!' is the age-old cry when a ship is sinking — it cannot be faulted, because it follows the first law. It suggests, too, that inner children must be listened to, cared for and cared about, and must not be lumbered with the responsibility of running our psychological lives. By implication, child abuse in any form is clearly a heinous crime. The foremost test for any social and political action is the legacy it will leave to coming generations.

• Next, the laws reveal some keys about how men and women may best relate to each other. The actual words are somewhat unfashionable, and to some perhaps a little old-fashioned, for they link the masculine principle with the idea of service and the feminine principle with the idea of surrender.

Please note: we say 'surrender', not 'give in'. The latter implies having no power, whereas the former cannot happen from a powerless position.

In practice we understand this law to mean that, in general, men have to learn to shift from being *in control* to *on patrol*. Men do have to change, even though they understandably long to be accepted and appreciated as they are. But for a man to undertake these changes in a guilty way, or while losing out on his sensitivity, would miss the point. The focus must be on developing his personal power. He will have to learn some mastery in his attitudes and handling of sexuality and aggression — but that is every man's task anyhow, so he might as well do it at home. He may even learn to be grateful to his partner for mirroring back his inner wheedling child or disguised tyrant.

Perhaps this sounds like hard work. But the first two principles do need an effort of will if they are to be honoured. But it does not have to be quite so heroic as it may sound, for there are payoffs. If a man reveres his inner feminine and takes on the lessons of relationship, he can develop a deeper masculinity than he ever dreamed of. Moreover, there is now a clear context for service. When in control shifts to on patrol there is a sense of being ever-watchful, of guarding the sacred, and decision-making (from the man's command centre rather than his control centre) becomes much easier. He just does whatever is needed!

Although most men do not start out with a natural flair for relationship, it can be learned – and it enormously enriches a man's life. It involves having some tolerance for pain, and the willingness to learn and to practise – like going to the gym and working out. If a man becomes a relationship yogi he may find that he receives much more loving and sex than he ever thought possible. Like the yogi, the man looks to his teacher (in this case his partner) to guide him to the lessons he needs, without giving over his power or projecting his authority onto her. The benefit is that there is a new part inside of him that awakes through this process and starts to govern his life, in service of his values.

- A woman, on the other hand, needs to learn to trust her own feminine power and to have confidence in herself. She needs only to be rooted in her deep feminine ground. A note of caution: this may sound easy, but she will have to make a big effort to put this into practice and to research appropriate role models. It will entail giving up projecting her power onto men, harbouring resentment and taking revenge on her children. When a woman knows in her being that she is empowered, then she can reach for the mirror and do her own psychological work – but it is hard to do it effectively before this has happened. But once she feels listened to and honoured, once she feels in possession of her own sovereignty and sees her partner doing conscious service to the first two principles, it is not just in her heart that she feels warm and relaxed! Knowing her own power and seeing the sacred laws observed, she can then naturally and lovingly surrender in the arms of her man.

- Finally, when the masculine and feminine energies reach their full and true potential an extraordinary alchemy takes place. The distinctions between them begin to melt away. Everything is different, but it looks just the same. And something wonderful is born, and reborn.

Surrendering – Relationship as Teacher

Is relationship then a spiritual path?

There are some resemblances, in that you have to commit to a practice, it makes you learn humility and eventually demands that you know how to surrender. It will indeed shake you and throw you around in the way that following a 'genuine' spiritual path does. It is certainly a sacred path, but it is not to be idealized. We would rather say that relationship can become a psychological and spiritual teacher, and has the ability to transform you, if you can bear to let it.

On such a path the teacher is the fiery aspect of God, in a way that the Sufis seem best to understand. Here is the thirteenth-century Sufi poet Rumi speaking about God as the Beloved:

I would love to kiss you
The price of kissing is your life

Now my love is running toward my life shouting,
What a bargain, let's buy it.[3]

On the path of relationship, the partner inevitably stands in for aspects of God and guru – although you might not recognize this, or thank them for performing that service for you. None of this is easy. It would be much preferable to have a teacher on a spiritual path, plus a village and a gender group, a shaman in the village, and elders and ancestors to hold you and guide you. It is hard to do it all on your own.

On this note, it is interesting how the teacher-student (or guru-disciple) relationship can mirror the relationship between intimate partners: the falling in love, the expectations of how a real teacher looks, behaves, talks and acts, then the disappointment and doubt when we find that the teacher/lover we encounter doesn't match what we expect. Rather than surrender our expectations, we are then tempted to go looking for a new teacher. It can be hard to trust that despite our fears, surrendering our hopes and expectations is what allows the real work to begin. What Sam Keen says here about spirituality could easily be said about relationships:

> At the heart of all spiritual experiences is the paradox of the mysterious marriage of choice and surrender, individual freedom and the acceptance of one's destiny.[4]

Surrender is not easy, whether on a spiritual path or in relationships. Before we can surrender we must inhabit a self which we think worth surrendering. Some degree of self-acceptance is needed before we can begin to face our fear of emptiness, which tends to grip us as we attempt to relinquish our habitual patterns of self-hatred, self-criticism and self-sabotage. In relationships we tend to transfer these negative feelings onto our partner, thereby maintaining the same preoccupation with non-acceptance. Our condemnation of the partner is the obsessive self-hatred of those aspects in ourselves. Giving it up would put us out of a job. It is often experienced as a sort of bereavement.

Our old identity has been our closest friend, our most intimate partner. Leaving it behind – which is what the extreme alchemy of relationship seems to demand – creates a void. It leaves us temporarily with an absence of company, like the absence of a shadow. It can be a terrifying experience. The internal sense of space and freedom is initially not recognized as such. We are more aware of the frightening experience of having no solid ground to anchor ourselves in. The loss of our identity as a fixed and solid entity causes our newfound ability to love to seem rather elusive.

To give up the idea of what we thought loving was and to commit to living with our partner is the kind of surrender which can only happen when we feel secure enough in our innate rightness. This has nothing to do with being perfect or having everything sorted out. It has more to do with a self-confidence that comes from having stopped fighting and made friends with ourselves, from having learned to love ourselves with all that we are, and granting the same grace to the partner. Once we can be secure in this way, we can surrender our idea of love. This is what we imagine the poet means when he says: he 'gave up loving, and lived with her'. The lines speak to a loss of illusion and a deep acceptance which yields a stronger love.

Here is Chögyam Trungpa Rinpoche, whose thoughts on disappointment we quoted at the beginning of this book, talking about this kind of surrender:

Surrendering is not a question of being low and stupid, nor of wanting to be elevated and profound. Instead, we surrender because we would like to communicate with the world 'as it is'. We know where we stand, therefore we make the gesture of surrendering, of opening, which means communication, link, direct communication with the object of our surrendering. We are not embarrassed about our rich collection of raw, rugged, beautiful and clean qualities. We present everything to the object of our surrendering.[5]

It was a warm Sunday afternoon. They were in the garage, tidying up the garden tools, a day after they had had one of their difficult nights.

She put down the shears, turned to him and quite without warning said. 'You know, I realize that it's been really difficult for me to be vulnerable with you. I've so needed you to be strong so that I could be soft. And you've let me down so often. I thought you were strong, but you weren't. And I've felt I had to do it all on my own.' She paused and looked at him, to see what his reaction was.

He, for his part, said nothing. He held her gaze, swallowed and leant back a bit against the wall.

'But that's my old, old story and I guess I never knew how to do it differently,' she continued. 'But today, I remembered that in so many other ways you've been supportive, in all kinds of things I never see. And I know you keep on doing them. So I want to thank you for that, I know you must feel that you never get appreciated...'

She saw how his eyes became moist and he breathed deeply.

'And all my life I've had to keep on without appreciation,' he said finally. 'I guess some of the things I've done were driven by that.'

So they went and weeded the garden.

After that, they found a private place, where the sweet grasses blew, and they made love.

CHAPTER 17
Living with Lust and Passion

Never too many fish in a swift creek
never too much water for fish to live in.
No place is too small for lovers,
nor can lovers see too much of the world.

Let the lover be disgraceful, crazy,
absentminded. Someone sober
will worry about events going badly.
Let the lover be.

A night full of talking that hurts,
my worst held-back secrets: Everything
has to do with loving and not loving.
This night will pass.
Then we have work to do.

Rumi[1]

William Blake said: 'If the fool would persist in his folly he
would become wise.'

And so it is for lovers too, we believe. Our final argument
– and the one that runs like a river through all the previous

chapters – is that falling in love is a message from the gods, from the soul. The messenger comes to us by way of all the trials we meet and must overcome *en route* towards each other.

The innocent fool in us falls in love and with this act opens the window to the soul. Suddenly we can see beyond the narrow boundaries of our egos; we experience love and bliss, and we like it. For a moment, the shadow aspects of our personality are kept out of the way. Selfishness, mistrust, fear, envy, jealousy, control give way to love. But this state does not last and these aspects reclaim their dominant place. Our insecurities and survival strategies take centre-stage again. We are then compelled to know and refine them, or live under their dominion.

Yet the experience of falling in love is not an illusion. By opening to love another soul we invoke the transpersonal source of love. But we are usually unprepared for the amount of spirit that enters. And, like most experiences involving spirit, it comes with a series of lessons. The deeper the connection between two people becomes, the more the psychological layers are revealed and have to be worked through. The combination of awakening the deepest parts in ourselves and sensing the possibility of relating from a fuller sense of self creates a tension. We are caught between the desire to follow our personal path and the demands of the relationship. This tension projects us into a new dimension where a different set of rules determines our actions.

All spiritual truths seem to be based on paradox, and paradoxes are hard to live. The path of relationship presents us with several different paradoxes, which are akin to the dilemmas we noticed earlier, except that they are pitched at a different level. These paradoxes include those of innocence and wisdom, love and work, consciousness and will, freedom of choice and commitment, 'beginner's mind' and maturity. These become our life-long allies and we are called to negotiate them with dignity, humility, discipline and humour.

Relationship Yoga

We have suggested that the lessons thrown up by living in an intimate relationship lead us into a pressure chamber for the development of our individual potential. The invitation is to whole-heartedly commit to the process. It is the hardest work; no wonder we need to be fooled into doing it.

The paradox between work and love is perhaps most easily identified in Hinduism, where there are two equally valued approaches to spiritual practice. One is yoga, meaning the harnessing of intent on a daily basis; the other is bhakti, meaning devotion, surrender to grace, or the ecstatic way of love. Yoga always stretches us but gets easier with practice; devotion reminds us that love is *ultimately* unconditional and accepting of limitation. Achieving bliss with any degree of permanence needs consciousness. Consciousness requires committed effort in order to pull stale and rigid patterns of being, thinking and doing into the light and release the energy for other uses.

In this context, all the issues and crises we encounter in our relationship can be seen as the raw material of soul work rather than a sign of not being right for each other. When the fool in us makes the choice to practise the yoga of relationship, the work of consciousness can begin.

With this recognition comes the need for mature responsibility, which paradoxically leads to a freer and deeper fulfilment. When awakening becomes the context, the old reference point of comfort is no longer so relevant. It can be hard work, but acceptance of our limitations, care and wonder about the other, as well as compassion and humour, ensure that love does not get lost in a mechanical heroism. Comfort, pleasure and joy may well arrive as by-products. Rilke has no doubt about the connection between work and love:

> There is scarcely anything more difficult than to love one another
> ... Like so much else, people have also misunderstood the place of
> love in life, they have made it into play and pleasure because they
> thought that play and pleasure were more blissful than work; but
> there is nothing happier than work, and love, just because it is
> the extreme happiness, can be nothing else but work. So whoever
> loves must try to act as if he had a great work...[2]

As with love, we may have to review our ideas of what work
is. In the Rilkean concept of work there is a certain amount of
ecstasy, of abandon – a lust for willing application! He pro-
claims it with utter passion. After all, having a partner is a
blessing. It is a state of grace to have someone with whom to
share the struggle to become whole, the task of learning how
to love; simply to share one's life.

Practising the yoga of relationship involves more joy than
expected. If you follow this path, you may be surprised to find
that you do not have to give up on (in fact you tend to get
rather a lot of):

friendship	power
love	commitment
affection	solitude
cuddles	clarity
flowers	creativity
champagne	minimum effort in return for maximum gain
sex	peace
passion	a sense of rightness to your life
disagreement	energy

You will, however, have to give up (or seriously cut down on):

your familiar safe distance for intimacy	blame
bonding patterns	guilt
the Pushme-Pullyou game	ambivalence
doing anything for a quiet life	self-pity
	co-dependence
addiction to conflict	survival patterns
tyranny	negativity
rage	thinking the grass is always greener
shame	addiction to misery

Could it be worth the effort?

Living with Each Other

When we have run around in bonding patterns, been parents and children to each other, pushed and pulled till we were exhausted, looked with horror and surprise and courage in the mirrors, yelled at each other and learned something about compassion through sharing our grief, after we have searched and found our gender identity, acknowledged our relationship as a third entity, raised children and spirit children and accepted death as part of life ... a transformed life dawns.

And then what?

Then we continue to live our everyday, ordinary lives.

Living together after renouncing our ideas of what love is may look just the same from the outside. But we have come a long way.

We start out identified as someone we are not, in order to be safe. Over the years, we discover more of who we are, but we don't recognize it as ourselves. Eventually, we relax into our new identity. The transformation does not create anything new. It simply awakens us to who we already are, but we have to get used to being ourselves and living naturally. And then there is the other. The projected image onto our partner is like a veil. When we remove it, the communication line is direct and clear – there is nothing in between us. There isn't any magic to it. The sense of magic comes from being open and available to live with oneself and each other, just as we are.

An extraordinary process of inner alchemy happens and ordinary life continues. It is a bit like the Zen saying:

> At first the mountains are mountains and the rivers are rivers. Then the mountains are not mountains and rivers are not rivers. But in the end mountains are mountains again and rivers are rivers again.

We still have to go to the supermarket for the shopping. We remain mortal and imperfect human beings; we do not transform into gods and goddesses. Instead we enter more deeply into the experience of being human, as T. S. Eliot reminds us:

> With the drawing of this Love
> and the voice of this Calling
> We shall not cease from exploration
> And the end of all our exploring
> Will be to arrive where we started
> And know the place for the first time.[3]

We are now available to enjoy living with each other. And this is where the lust and passion comes in. Two adults dancing to the tune of love are very real. They make their desires known and can also say 'no'. Pleasing the other is less important than honesty. Disagreements are not swept under the carpet and feelings can flow freely.

To begin with this kind of relationship seems like hard work, but then something happens, and it is not. We are carried by a desire to become the best we are, for our own sake. What we do and who we are is no longer *for* the other, or even for the relationship. Instead it becomes *for* ourselves, yet *about* the other and the relationship. When this becomes natural, relationship is very simple. You can relax a bit. The inevitable ups and downs are but the tiresome yet necessary tasks of housekeeping. They are part of life. This is the time when the relationship pays back for all the effort and commitment, when the maturity of having raised a Third Being is like the maturity of having raised children.

It reminds us of a story we were once told about a man who spent hours at sea, sharing his passion for sailing with his young sons. Despite many potentially dangerous moments on the waves, each time his skill and attention had supported his total commitment to get them home safely. Time passed and one day they hit a storm which proved too much for him. But his sons, who were now grown, buckled to. As he watched them take charge, working together with skill and determination, he wept. He recognized that something had come to an end. He had made his last trip with all the responsibility on his shoulders. He was no longer alone on the high seas.

Passion and Sex in Long-Term Relationships

Living with lust and passion is an attitude to life and not a style; it is not exclusively about sex, but it includes it. Since it is not always easy to keep the passion going in long-term relationships, we want to speak a little about love-making before finishing.

Sex is the celebration of intimacy – but it is also the place where many of our emotional and relational problems come out.

While the mass media remains obsessed with unrealistic bodily perfection and immature concepts of sexuality, in many houses fear, shame and ignorance are connected to the idea of making love. Whenever sexuality remains fixed on a mental image we stay isolated in our own minds and risk falling either into avoidance or an addictive pattern of needing increasingly exciting stimulus to reach any satisfaction. Similarly, if our sexuality becomes the only outlet for our wildest and most creative impulses, what we are looking for (and what nourishes us) will keep eluding us.

We consider sexual intimacy as *primarily* relational, secondly physical. Bodies rarely have problems finding sexual pleasure if the confusion in the mind is laid to rest. Being sexually alive has little to do with the right body shape, or the right partner. It is about one's self-concept, self-embodiment and attitude to life, and the ability to reprogramme internal messages from the image-makers of the past. Living life fully, with lust and passion, is the best foundation for men and women to come together in joyful and conscious pleasure. Being 'turned on' by life allows our sexual activities to be the natural expression of that enjoyment.

In everyday life, however, when faced with commitments to children, jobs, financial demands and so on, it can become easy to let your passion, your sexuality and your care for the Third Being slip away. It is crucial to create times in your life to remember *why* you are together. If *you* are always last on the list there won't be time for each other, for passion, to go beyond what you previously might have settled for. Remember, when passion arises – such as in a new affair – people always find time to fit it in. It's a bit like the old saying 'To get a job done, ask a busy person'. This is important for all couples, but especially if you have children.

We can usefully think of the amount of sexual energy between partners as a charge between opposite poles, as in magnetism. This can be seen in couples who, through their addiction to conflict, can develop a lot of charge, which they use in their sex life. It may excite them for a while, but it is unlikely to be a connection which builds intimacy. Excitement and charge inevitably change over time.

In the classic case, where the male is more genitally charged than the female, a natural change starts to come in at middle age. Here men have a tendency to become passive and less interested in sex, and women the reverse. A man who is already in retreat from sex and the dangers of intimacy may then begin to wither. In fact, on a physical level, the penis of an ageing man who is not sexually active can literally retract back into his body.

Some couples who are afraid of conflict and of polarizing find that there is so little charge between them that they are too bored for sex to happen. A man once told us:

> Sex is something you do and then it's done, thank God. I know – roughly – what to do with my genitals, but beyond that I'm not really sure what I want.

But here all is not lost. If he and his partner could build on his passionate honesty and shine the healing power of his humour into their bed, they would have a good starting-point for a potentially enjoyable adventure!

Mature couples can actually have the best sex of their lives, if they understand the possibilities open to them. Both need to have cultivated an open heart and some awareness and skill of genital sensitivity. Just as men need to learn to be open-hearted during love-making, to be guided by their hearts, women need to learn to support the love in their hearts with the heat in their genitals. In other words, men must learn to have their penetrative potency rooted in a strong and softened heart, and women to have their love and care informed by the fire from their genitals. In this way men can express loving lust; women can become lustful lovers.

In cases of too much or too little charge between a couple, time alone can recharge the relationship in a more balanced way and build a stock of good memories. To prevent a new impasse, the couple will need to cultivate the commitment to support each other. Occasionally, couples try to revive their flagging passions by experimenting with 'open' relationships, where both are free to have sex and intimacy with other partners. At best, this is an attempt to express love without possessiveness, but mostly the reality of such arrangements is far from idyllic. We have not yet met a couple who could sustain this tension without one of the partners sacrificing their needs on the altar of freedom. In general, the child inside each partner cannot deal with it. Usually the relationship breaks up in the end, often with guilt about not being able to handle these things better. Subsequently, each person tends to seek out a partner who wants to commit to a monogamous relationship.

Ripening with Grace

Do some couples bypass the stages we have described and yet reach real contentment? Who can judge? No relationship is perfect, but there are people who seem to have been born with a talent for love. Perhaps they don't get stuck anywhere too long, or they trust the cycle of life and death and are secure enough in their identity to live with the differences in their partner. Maturity must have a part to play in such cases, along with its paradoxical partner, innocence. Lessons learned from previous relationships also help in knowing different steps. Sometimes people fall in love later in life and the relationship they have already developed with themselves can mean that they are ready to embrace and celebrate the differences the other presents.

One such couple has been an inspiration to us. Helena first met them when she was three years old. Alfred was a bachelor farmer in a little fishing village on the Baltic coast of Denmark. Riding high on the hay of his horse-drawn wagon, he had no trouble recommending that the family that one day turned up in a Volkswagen van should park in his newly harvested field and put up a couple of tents. He was that kind of a man. This began a friendship and a tradition of summer holidays that spanned several generations.

At the other end of the village lived Fru Malling, the district midwife. This proud, statuesque lady, who always wore her hair up, was never addressed informally ('Fru' is Danish for 'Mrs' or 'Madame'). Meeting her on her daily bicycle ride through the village was like greeting royalty. Yet she was warm and friendly. The strength of her personality and her quiet yet powerful composure gave her a natural aura of authority.

Increasingly, over the years, Fru Malling and Alfred were seen together – he in his shabby sleeveless pullover and shapeless trousers, with a glint in his eye under his weathered straw hat and his dry, teasing comments; she, immaculately dressed and impeccably mannered, ever ready with proud, yet fond rebukes. And then one summer, when Alfred was 79 and Fru Malling 80, they sent out wedding invitations.

The ceremony took place at a registry office, Alfred, in a suit for the first time in his life, as dapper and proud as any young man ready to claim his bride, and Fru Malling blushing and shy under her big-brimmed hat. When they kissed to seal their commitment, it was the guests who blushed. The passion between them was unmistakable. The time came for Alfred to make his speech at the reception in the modest inn. Making sure he had the attention of his audience, he turned to his wife and calmly said:

I have never been one for making hasty decisions. I like to take my time over important things and marriage is important to me. I never doubted your worth in all the years we courted. But it has taken me till now before I was sure that my love was worthy of you. I no longer doubt that. We are not young anymore, but the way I feel today and what I see when I look at you, makes me question what it means to be young. I can think of nothing that makes me happier than your promise today to spend the rest of your life with me, as my wife.

They had 20 years together and though neither had ever been abroad before they travelled to China, Russia, India and many places in Europe. They lived in Fru Malling's cottage, ten feet from the waters of the gentle Baltic, until the end of their days.

The last time we visited, Alfred greeted us with an apology. He couldn't shake hands, for they were covered in dough. He was making the weekly batch of home-made bread, but looked sad and tired. Malling, as he now intimately called her, had died a few weeks before, days after turning 100. 'She always knew she would die at that age,' he said.

We had some good years together. We never imagined that we would be given so many years, so we decided to do exactly what we wanted every day. And the days kept coming, so we got pretty good at it. Now, while I get the glasses, you tell your man what I've been saying. He doesn't understand much of our language, does he?

Alfred died little over a year later, having just turned 100.

Conscious Relationship as a Vision for the Future

It's easy to believe that only special and important people have the power to make any lasting mark on history. We are convinced that this is not the case. Leaving all the responsibility to our political or spiritual leaders is only an echo of expecting our parents or partners to make it all better. It can give us an excuse to blame, but in the final analysis, it simply allows us to sign away responsibility for the coming generations.

Adolescents naturally look to the famous and beautiful for role models, as idealized images in their search for identity. But unless this is backed by the experience of contact with ordinary men and women whom they admire and are excited by, it won't sustain them in living a rich and purposeful life. Young people have an urgent hunger for those who are not afraid of life, sex and relationships. They are affected by us and how we 'walk our talk' in everyday life impacts them; even unspoken messages are passed on to our children and the young people we meet. If we can go beyond the epidemic of separation and resignation in relationships to discover something valuable, then our young people have a chance to feel anchored.

When couples find a purpose to their struggle, the work they do can be transformative. It may not be too much to propose that if this could happen *en masse*, humanity might discover a new key, a new solution, which could be as life-changing as the information revolution. We all co-create tomorrow's world. The vision we hold and how we apply our skills will determine whether the unresolved issues of countless generations may be redeemed and whether the excessive passing on of the 'sins of the fathers' may be stemmed.

It matters how we live our lives.

And Finally...

We are under no illusion that reading this book will magically have transformed your relationship and your life. If that were possible, we would all be enlightened by now, considering the amount of wise words in print. To understand a process is one thing. To live it is altogether another matter. And the only way to realize what living with lust and passion means is to do it.

We must, however, admit to a final hope: that what we have shared will go some way in allowing couples to trust the power and wisdom in the processes which their love presents them with. We hope that creatively surrendering to it will eventually empower and enlighten them, that they will experience their ordinary yet unique lives turning into fertile soil in which they may bring their potential to full bloom and their deepest visions to fruition.

Our future, and that of coming generations, may depend on us daring to live our dreams awake.

'I don't believe it!' he gasped under his breath when he found the cheque he had been looking for all evening — in its envelope in the waste paper bin under the desk.

Of course he had thrown it there himself, but he didn't expect cheques to be in their envelopes. So he marched into the living-room, flushed both with indignation and excitement.

The room was bathed in a warm light, which came from the fire, the candles and the old tasselled lamp. When he saw her sitting in the armchair, reading her book, surrounded by the notes she had made, a glass of wine and the cat at her side, he faltered. His heart softened, he could hardly breathe; he felt both light and anchored.

So he approached silently, kissed her from behind, tenderly on the back of her neck and went back to the study.

Whether she noticed how he had entered — or even left — the room, you would not be able to say.

After all, the room was warm and dark, and the evening was too lovely to waste.

Endnote

If you would like more information on therapy and workshops for couples and retreats for men and women in gender groups, as well as further publications, please visit Helena and Nick's website:

www.genderpsychology.com

Those with a professional interest in training for couple workers, supervision, gender psychology or sexuality training are also directed to the site.

If you would like to enquire about the possibility of the authors offering a lecture, seminar or consultation in your area, please e-mail them at:

info@genderpsychology.com

Notes

Chapter 1

1 Susan Edwards, *When Men Believe in Love*, Element Books, Shaftesbury, 1995

2 Robert Bly, extract from 'Listening to the Köln Concert', *Loving a Woman in Two Worlds*, Doubleday, 1985

Chapter 2

1 *The Times*, 6 February 1988, quoted in Tony Gough, *Couples in Counselling*, Darton, Longman and Todd, London, 1989

2 *Independent on Sunday*, 9 January 2000

3 Quoted in Caroline Sullivan, 'Together Apart', *Guardian*, 4 September 2000

4 Quoted ibid

5 Tony Parsons, *Man and Boy*, HarperCollins, London, 1999

6 Ibid

7 Polly Vernon, 'You've Lost that Loving Feeling', *Guardian*, 23 October 2000

8 *Who's Afraid of the Ten Commandments? The Seventh Commandment*, chaired by Melvyn Bragg, Channel Four, 1999

9 Ibid

Chapter 3

1 Cole Porter, *I've got you under my skin*, © 1973 Chappell Co., Inc., assigned to Buxton Hill Music Corp., USA, Warner/Chappell Music Ltd

2 *Independent*, September 1993
3 J. G. Frazer, *The Golden Bough: A Study in Magic and Religion*, Macmillan Press, London, 1922
4 Jean-Luc Toussaint, *The Walnut Cookbook*, trans. B. Draine and M. Hinden, Ten Speed Press, Berkeley, CA, 1998

Chapter 4

1 Barry Mann, Cynthia Weil and Phil Spector, *You've Lost That Lovin' Feelin'* © 1964, 1965 (renewed 1992, 1993) Screen Gems-EMI Music, Inc., and Mother Bertha Music, Inc., administered by ABKCO Music, Inc.
2 Subonfu Somé, *The Spirit of Intimacy*, Berkeley Hills Books, Berkeley, CA, 1997
3 Chögyam Trungpa, *Cutting Through Spiritual Materialism*, Shambala, Boston and London, 1973. We have taken the liberty of translating the word *Dharma* as 'Truth'
4 Tony Parsons, *Man and Boy*, HarperCollins, London, 1999
5 Ellen J. Clephane, *Dance of Love*, Element Books, Shaftesbury, 1995

Chapter 5

1 Bill Holm, 'Advice', *The Dead Get by with Everything*, Milkweed Editions, Minneapolis, 1990
2 Nick Hornby, *About a Boy*, HarperCollins, London, 1998
3 Sam Keen, *Fire in the Belly*, Bantam Books, New York, 1991
4 From a survey done in 1993, reported in the *Independent*, 29 September 1993
5 Tony Parsons, *Man and Boy*, HarperCollins, London, 1999

Chapter 6

1 We have written elsewhere how this interplay between these needs is structured in a precise hierarchy and how precarious this balancing act can become. *See* Nick Duffell, *The Making of Them*, Lone Arrow Press, London, 2000
2 The classic text is Thomas Fogarty, 'The distancer and the pursuer', *The Family* 7, 1 (1979), 11–16
3 Maggie Scarf, *Intimate Partners*, Century Hutchinson, London, 1987
4 Dudley Young, *Origins of the Sacred*, Abacus, London, 1993. This remark comes from a talk at The Soho Laundry, London, 1995

5 Sheldon Kopp, *If You Meet the Buddha on the Road, Kill Him!*, Sheldon Press, 1979

6 Scarf, op. cit.

7 S. J. Betchen and J. L. Ross, 'Male pursuers and female distancers in couples therapy', *Journal of the British Association for Sexual and Relationship Therapy* 15, 1 (2000)

8 Tony Gough, *Couples in Counselling*, Darton, Longman and Todd, London, 1989

Chapter 7

1 *See* Jean Liedloff, *The Continuum Concept*, Arkana, London, 1986

2 *See* Nick's *The Making of Them*, Lone Arrow Press, London, 2000

3 *See* the theories of internal objects of W. D. Fairbairn, especially as described in Stephen M. Johnson's masterpiece, *Character Styles*, W. W. Norton, New York, 1994

4 *See* Eric Berne's *The Games People Play*, Grove Press, New York, 1964

5 *See* H. Stone and S. Winkleman, *Embracing Each Other*, New World Library, San Rafael, CA, 1989

Chapter 8

1 Felix Pollak, 'The Dream', *Subject to Change*, Juniper Press, 1978

Chapter 9

1 Roger McGough, 'First Degree Marriage', *After the Merrymaking*, Jonathan Cape, London, 1971

2 Edward Goldwyn, 'The Fight to be Male', *The Listener*, 24 May 1979. Thanks to Erica Moss for making us aware of this article

3 Ibid

4 R. R. Greenson, 'Dis-identifying from mother: its special importance for the boy', *International Journal of Psycho-Analysis* 49, 370 (1968)

5 L. Hudson and B. Jacot, *The Way Men Think*, Yale University Press, Newhaven and London, 1991

6 L. Hudson and B. Jacot, *Intimate Relations*, Yale University Press, Newhaven and London, 1995

7 Christiane Olivier, *Jocasta's Children: The Imprint of the Mother*, Routledge, London, 1989

8 Michael Meade, from a talk given at The Soho Factory, London, 1995

Chapter 10

1 John Gray, *Men are from Mars, Women are from Venus*, Thorsons, London, 1993

2 Ronald Taffel, 'Why is Daddy so Grumpy?', *Women and Power: Perspectives for Family Therapy*, ed. T. J. Goodrich, W. W. Norton, New York, 1991, quoted Elsa Jones and Eisa Asen's quite excellent *Systemic Couple Therapy and Depression*, Karnac Books, London, 2000

3 *See* Marion Woodman, *Addiction to Perfection*, Inner City Books, Toronto, 1982

4 Bill Holm, 'Advice', *The Rag and Bone Shop of the Heart*, eds. Robert Bly, James Hillman and Michael Meade, Harper Perennial, New York, 1993

Chapter 11

1 We have adapted some of the excellent terminology outlined by Susan Edwards in *When Men Believe in Love*, Element Books, Shaftesbury, 1995

2 Thanks to Robert Bly for making these stages clear

3 Sam Keen, *Fire in the Belly*, Bantam Books, USA, 1991

4 Mario Jacoby, *Shame and the Origins of Self-esteem*, Routledge, London, 1994

Chapter 12

1 D. H. Lawrence, 'Intimates', *The Love Poems of D. H. Lawrence*, ed. Roy Booth, Kylie Cathie, London, 1993

2 *See* Nick's *The Making of Them*, Lone Arrow Press, London, 2000

3 Quoted in A. C. Grayling, *The Quarrel of an Age* (a biography of Hazlitt), Weidenfeld & Nicolson, London, 2000

4 James Holis, *The Eden Project*, Inner City Books, New York, 1998

5 Quoted by Robert Young in *Mental Space*, Process Press, London, 1994

6 Chris Robertson, 'ReVisioning', *Journal of ReVision*, 11 (1998), Centre for Integrative Psychosynthesis, London. Thanks to Dorry Ender for making us aware of both this and the third of our quotations in this chapter

7 Those interested in this issue should see H. G. Learner's *The Dance of Intimacy*, Thorsons, London, 1990, particularly the section 'The Will Not to Change', and W. D. Fairbairn's theories of attachment to Bad Objects, best explained by S. M. Johnson in *Character Styles*, W. W.

Norton, New York, 1994. For a further powerful explanation *see* Harley SwiftDeer Reagan's 'The Teaching of the Seven Arrows' in *Shamanic Wheels and Keys*, DTMMS, Scottsdale, AR, 1980

Chapter 13
1 Robert Bly, 'Listening to the Köln Concert', *Loving a Woman in Two Worlds*, Doubleday, 1985
2 Clarissa Pinkola Estes, *Women Who Run with the Wolves*, Rider, London, 1992
3 Hal Stone and Sidra Winkleman, *Embracing Each Other*, New World Library, San Rafael, CA, 1989
4 For this quotation and the brilliantly simple but powerful formulation 'How do *I* have difficulties in loving?' we owe thanks to Stanley Keleman. *See* his *Love: A Somatic View*, Centre Press, Berkeley, CA, 1994
5 Polly Young-Eisendrath, *Hags and Heroes*, Inner City Books, New York, 1984. Thanks to Lynne Hunter for making us aware of this passage
6 Thomas Moore, *Soul Mates: Honouring the Mysteries of Love and Relationship*, Element Books, Shaftesbury, 1994

Chapter 14
1 Clarissa Pinkola Estes, *Women Who Run with the Wolves*, Rider, London, 1992
2 Henry David Thoreau, *Walden*, Penguin Books, London, 1984
3 Thomas Moore, *Soul Mates*, Element Books, Shaftesbury, 1994
4 Rainer Maria Rilke, *Rilke on Love and Other Difficulties*, complied and translated by J. J. L. Mood, W. W. Norton, New York, 1975

Chapter 15
1 Robert Bly, 'A Man and a Woman Sit Near Each Other', *Loving a Woman in Two Worlds*, Doubleday, 1985
2 We imagine that this may be as true for homosexual couples as it is for heterosexuals, but we do not pretend any authority in those areas
3 David L. Miller, *Three Faces of God: The Traces of the Trinity in Literature and Life*, Fortress Press, Philadelphia, 1986, quoted by Thomas Moore in *Soul Mates: Honouring the Mysteries of Love and Relationship*, Element Books, Shaftesbury, 1994
4 A great example of this issue is portrayed in the last work of the master film-maker Stanley Kubric, *Eyes Wide Shut*. *See* our 'Sex,

power, and spirit: jottings from a humanistic notebook', *Self & Society* 29, 2, June–July 2000

Chapter 16

1 Robert Creeley, 'A Marriage', *Collected Poems of Robert Creeley 1945–1975*, University of California Press, 1983
2 We would like here to honour and thank Harley SwiftDeer Reagan for his wise teachings
3 Jalal al-Din Rumi, 'Open Secret', *Versions of Rumi*, translated by John Moyne and Coleman Barks, Threshold Books, Putney, Vermont, 1984
4 Sam Keen, *Fire in the Belly*, Bantam Books, New York, 1991
5 Chögyam Trungpa, *Cutting through Spiritual Materialism*, Shambhala, Boston and London, 1973

Chapter 17

1 Jalal al-Din Rumi, 'Three Quatrains', translated by John Moyne and Coleman Barks, *Unseen Rain*, Threshold Books, Putney, Vermont, 1986
2 Rainer Maria Rilke, *Rilke on Love and Other Difficulties*, complied and translated by J. J. L. Mood, W. W. Norton, New York, 1975
3 T. S. Eliot, 'Little Gidding', *Four Quartets*, Faber & Faber, London, 1944

Bibliography

Berne, E., *The Games People Play*, Grove Press, New York, 1964

Betchen, S. J., and Ross, J. L., 'Male pursuers and female distancers in couples therapy', *Journal of the British Association for Sexual and Relationship Therapy* 15, 1 (2000)

Bly, R., *Loving a Woman in Two Worlds*, Doubleday, 1985

Bly, R., Hillman, J., Meade, M. (eds), *The Rag and Bone Shop of the Heart*, Harper Perennial, New York, 1993

Clephane, E. J., *Dance of Love*, Element Books, Shaftesbury, 1995

Creeley, R., *Collected Poems of Robert Creeley 1945–75*, University of California Press, 1983

Duffell, N., *The Making of Them*, Lone Arrow Press, London, 2000

Duffell, N., and Løvendal Sørensen, H., 'Sex, power, and spirit: jottings from a humanistic notebook', *Self & Society* 29, 2, June–July 2000

—, 'Professional, personal and private: the challenge of working creatively with couples', *Self & Society* 27, 4, August–September 1999

—, 'Dancing in the dark: from conflict to compassion in intimate relationships', *Human Potential*, Winter 1996/7

Edwards, S., *When Men Believe in Love*, Element Books, Shaftesbury, 1995

Eliot, T. S., *Four Quartets*, Faber & Faber, London, 1944

Estes, C. P., *Women Who Run with the Wolves*, Rider, London, 1992

Fogarty, T., 'The distancer and the pursuer', *The Family* 7, 1 (1979), 11–16

Frazer, J. G., *The Golden Bough: A Study in Magic and Religion*, Macmillan Press, London, 1922

Goldwyn, E., 'The Fight to be Male', *The Listener*, 24 May 1979

Gough, T., *Couples in Counselling*, Darton, Longman and Todd, London, 1989

Grayling, A. C., *The Quarrel of an Age*, Weidenfeld & Nicolson, London, 2000

Greenson, R. R., 'Dis-identifying from mother: its special importance for the boy', *International Journal of Psycho-Analysis* 49, 370 (1968)

Holis, J., *The Eden Project*, Inner City Books, New York, 1998

Hornby, N., *About a Boy*, HarperCollins, London, 1998

Housden R., and Goodchild, C., *We Two*, Aquarian/Thorsons, London, 1992

Hudson, L., and Jacot, B., *The Way Men Think*, Yale University Press, Newhaven and London, 1991

—, *Intimate Relations*, Yale University Press, Newhaven and London, 1995

Jacoby, M., *Shame and the Origins of Self-esteem*, Routledge, London, 1994

Johnson, S. M., *Character Styles*, W. W. Norton, New York, 1994

Jones E., and Asen, E., *Systemic Couple Therapy and Depression*, Karnac Books, London, 2000

Keen, S., *Fire in the Belly*, Bantam Books, New York, 1991

Keleman, S., *Love: A Somatic View*, Centre Press, Berkeley, CA, 1994

Klein, J., *Our Need for Others and its Roots in Infancy*, Tavistock, London, 1987

Kopp, S., *If You Meet the Buddha on the Road, Kill Him!*, Sheldon Press, 1979

Lawrence, D. H., *The Love Poems of D. H. Lawrence*, ed. Roy Booth, Kylie Cathie, London, 1993

Learner, H. G., *The Dance of Intimacy*, Thorsons, London, 1990

Liedloff, J., *The Continuum Concept*, Arkana, London, 1986

Miller, D. L., *Three Faces of God: The Traces of the Trinity in Literature and Life*, Fortress Press, Philadelphia, 1986

Moore, T., *Soul Mates: Honouring the Mysteries of Love and Relationship*, Element Books, Shaftesbury, 1994

Olivier, C., *Jocasta's Children: The Imprint of the Mother*, Routledge, London, 1989

Parsons, T., *Man and Boy*, HarperCollins, London, 1999

Reagan, H. S. D., *Shamanic Wheels and Keys*, DTMMS, Scottsdale, AR, 1980

Rilke, R. M., *Rilke on Love and Other Difficulties*, compiled and translated by J. J. L. Mood, W. W. Norton, New York, 1975

Robertson, C., 'ReVisioning', *Journal of ReVision* 11, Centre for Integrative Psychosynthesis, London, 1998

Rumi, Jalal al-Din, 'Open Secret', *Versions of Rumi*, translated by John Moyne and Coleman Barks, Threshold Books, Putney, Vermont, 1984

—, *Unseen Rain*, translated by John Moyne and Coleman Barks, Threshold Books, Putney, Vermont, 1986

Scarf, M., *Intimate Partners*, Century Hutchinson, London, 1987

Somé M. P., *Of Water and the Spirit*, Tarcher Putnam, New York, 1994

Somé, S., *The Spirit of Intimacy*, Berkeley Hills Books, Berkeley, CA, 1997

Stern, D., *The Interpersonal World of the Infant*, Basic Books, New York, 1985

Stone, H., and Winkleman, S., *Embracing Each Other*, New World Library, San Rafael, CA, 1989

Taffel, R., 'Why is Daddy so grumpy?', *Women and Power: Perspectives for Family Therapy*, ed. T. J. Goodrich, W. W. Norton, New York, 1991

Thoreau, H. D., *Walden*, Penguin Books, London, 1984

Toussaint, J-L., *The Walnut Cookbook*, trans. B. Draine and M. Hinden, Ten Speed Press, Berkeley, CA, 1998

Trungpa, C., *Cutting through Spiritual Materialism*, Shambhala, Boston, 1973

Woodman, M., *Addiction to Perfection*, Inner City Books, Toronto, 1982

Young, D., *Origins of the Sacred*, Abacus, London, 1993

Young, R., *Mental Space*, Process Press, London, 1994

Young-Eisendrath, P., *Hags and Heroes*, Inner City Books, New York, 1984

triggers to acting out?
Suppress inner child, promote inner adult

KJ + DM p 80 - co-dependency

KJ - What is C saying when he wants u to be more needy?
→ he wants to feel more manly
→ but he's out of his depth when it comes
   to serious needs — makes him feel vuln.
   + yr role is to protect him
   (f. dad c 14)
C blaming her for him having the affair — ie she's
                                    not 'needy' enough
KJ - Peter Pan will have to grow   of him
        up, but wendy will have to let him

129 polarsaton - only 2 options?

189 Q - How do I have difficulties loving?